PELLEGRINO RICCARDI

Drowning
Quietly

MEMOIR OF A
MAN'S SHORTCOMINGS

RIVER GROVE
BOOKS

This book is a memoir reflecting the author's present recollections of experiences over time. Its story and its words are the author's alone. Some details and characteristics may be changed, some events may be compressed, and some dialogue may be recreated.

Published by River Grove Books
Austin, TX
www.rivergrovebooks.com

Distributed by River Grove Books

Design and composition by Greenleaf Book Group and Brian Phillips
Cover design by Greenleaf Book Group and Brian Phillips

Cover images copyright Alena Ohneva and Naoki Kim
Used under license from Shutterstock.com

Publisher's Cataloging-in-Publication data is available.

Print ISBN: 978-1-63299-506-3

eBook ISBN: 978-1-63299-507-0

First Edition

A man has only one escape from his old self, and that is to see a different self in the mirror of some woman's eyes.

—Clare Boothe Luce, *The Women*

Contents

Preface

The catalyst for this book was an event that happened on a hot summer's day in the south of Italy when I left my three-year-old daughter, Olivia, alone by the pool. You never know just how fragile life can be until the loss of it is thrust in your face, out of nowhere, without warning, and without mercy.

That fateful summer's day was life changing. It forced me to look at myself again, to see who I really was. Most importantly, it compelled me to examine the man that I had become—a man who, among many other shortcomings, would leave his daughter alone by a pool.

Steve Jobs once said that "you can't connect the dots looking forward; you can only connect them looking backwards."[1] This book is an attempt to connect those dots—but not all the dots. No, the dots that I am going to focus on are those that say something about me as a man. Specifically, the man I am *in relation to women*.

---

1   Steve Jobs, Stanford University commencement speech, June 12, 2005, Stanford, CA, available at https://www.youtube.com/watch?v=sFaLN4xITTI.

I didn't like the man I saw when I observed him in the mirror, the man who'd abandoned his daughter by a pool. I needed to see a new man, a new self so that, if nothing else, at least I could forgive myself for being the man I was. I needed to escape from the airbrushed self that people see on my Facebook and LinkedIn pages. That's not me. That man appears to have many of the trappings of success, but they are just smoke screens, designed to divert people away from the truth, which is that he is filled with insecurity, vulnerability, and weaknesses.

One of the things this book will do is blow away those smoke screens and reveal some of the more painful truths that I live with every day—not only *my* truths but the truths of many a man out there. You see, I am of the conviction that many men feel the same as I do: that we are wandering about behind a smoke screen of self-deception and self-doubt. We are lost, aimless, incompetent, not thinking straight, and acting as if we are in control when we know we are not at all.

That summer's day in Italy proved to me, at least, that we are *definitely* not in control. And only when I began seeing myself in the mirror of women's eyes did I begin to see who I truly was and who I wanted to be. In my case, those women were my mother, my wife, and my two daughters.

I have made the decision to tell you nearly everything, to make myself as naked and as vulnerable as the day when the doctors cut my umbilical cord in St. Martin's Hospital in Bath, UK, on October 7, 1964, and handed me over to my mother's waiting arms. I ask you to handle me with as much care as my mother did that day. The stories you are about to read are very personal. I have written them as if no one is reading. In other words, they are open and unapologetically honest. I'm opening up my inner thoughts to you. I'm inviting you into my mind so that you can peer at all my fears, all my shortcomings, all my vulnerabilities, and all my weaknesses. Please go easy on me.

Naturally, I hope that the stories will resonate with you, the reader. I think they will especially resonate with male readers. But my hope is that women readers too will read this book and come to an understanding, perhaps even a *better* understanding, that we men are no less vulnerable and fragile than they are—because we are. I know that I am not the only man who feels this.

I hope men will read this book and feel confident enough to be more open with others about their feelings, about their vulnerabilities, and about their failures—*especially* their failures. That's what this book will be focusing on: failures—as a man, as a husband, and as a father. That focus is not because I like to beat myself up or because I am looking for your pity or sympathy but because I know that the only way to extinguish the fire of shame that hangs over me is to expose it. Shame feeds on secrecy. But if you remove the secrecy, you also remove the fuel that keeps shame alive. And the best part of all, you become stronger for it afterward.

So, I invite you to read my story with an open mind and an open heart—especially your heart. Cry with me, and laugh with me—because I believe you may well do both. And if you don't want to laugh with me, then laugh *at* me. That's fine too, as long as you remain open minded and open hearted all the way to the final page.

Finally, I hope that this book provides you with what I call *the three Es*: It entertains you, it educates you, and it elevates you.

"Life is like a cup of espresso: You have to have the bitter and the sweet." That's what my mother used to say. You have to taste the bitterness of the coffee with the sweetness of the sugar. And the more bitter experiences of life often teach us the most.

I know that this was certainly the case on that summer's day in Italy.

Lommedalen, Norway
March 2022

Prologue

Two arctic blue eyes strain to focus through the blurry chlorine water on the image at the bottom of the pool. Like any three-year-old, the little girl has no idea what she needs, only what she wants, and what she *wants* right now is to find out what that drawing at the bottom of the pool is.

Just a couple of weeks ago, she'd drawn a picture just like that on the bathroom floor back home in Norway. She loved making pictures. The house was covered in them. On the walls, on the doors, behind her headboard, on the Norwegian wood floors, even in the bathtub. They were smiley faces, spiders, and houses with crooked windows and lopsided chimneys that looked like they would topple off their roofs at any moment. She loved drawing stars, even though she could never get all the sides to be of equal length. She never understood why her father got so angry with her when she drew stars on the wall. She was always careful to use a pencil.

"I would never use a felt tip pen, Pappa," she told her father earnestly, to which he muttered something about pencils being just as difficult to get off walls as a felt tip pen. Obviously, Pappa's eraser wasn't as good as the one she used at school, she thought.

So, when she sees that sketch on the bottom of the pool, she is immediately drawn to it. Who on earth could have drawn a picture on the bottom of the pool? Whoever it was must have used a felt tip. *I bet that child's Pappa got angry too*, she thinks. But what is it a picture *of* exactly? Without her goggles on, it is hard to focus and make out what the drawing is. She needs to get closer.

As she inches her delicate feet down the slope of the pool, she begins to make out that it is not a drawing at all but a puzzle. It's a jigsaw puzzle of tiny multicolored ceramic tiles of all shapes and sizes, shimmering beneath the water in the hot Italian sun. But it's hard to make out what it is *of*. Is it a fish? A dolphin? A mermaid perhaps?

If her father had been there, he would have told her it was called a *mosaic*. She may even have repeated the word back to him: *mo-say-ick*.

She moves toward the image, calmly descending a little more into the water. She feels no concern or agitation. Why should a child feel agitated when she knows that her mother and father are close at hand to keep her safe? And normally, that would indeed be the case. But not today.

Today, this girl is alone. Today, she is a solo Norwegian adventurer on a perilous expedition to a primeval water world that spawned the first forms of life, a place from which humans emerged but where they no longer belong. For the time being, her primeval memory reminds her to block her trachea so that she doesn't swallow the chlorinated pool water.

She passes below the overhanging branch of the olive tree, an ancient Apulian olive tree that has stood there for over a hundred years. It was the one tree that was not cut down when the owners of the converted farmhouse decided to build a swimming pool there. They'd wanted to keep a solitary symbolic reminder of what the property used to look like before middle class families like hers began spending their holidays here.

Below the waterline, the little girl begins to sense what she needs, not just what she wants. Her tiny lungs will soon need air. Those lungs are no bigger than the birthday balloons her father hung up for her on the beams of the poolside pergola just the day before, and they are starting to burn like the candles on her cake.

Like any three-year-old child would do, she raises her arms in the universal symbol of "up." Those two small arms reach above the silky waterline, slicing gently through the surface like twin fleshy periscopes.

A drooping branch of the ancient olive tree reaches feebly down toward her like an old man trying to do up his laces. A meter of void now divides her outstretched hands and the crooked fingertips of the olive branch. If only that ancient olive could reach down and take her hand, lift her to safety. If only that branch were as young and supple as that child. Then it could stretch a little farther, all the way down to the glistening waterline. It could hold out a small olive leaf of hope for Olivia to grab on to—a leaf of hope.

Her father and mother named her Olivia because she was a symbol of hope, of life. Olivia's older brother and sister had been made in a petri dish, but Olivia had been conceived naturally, against all odds. She had breathed new life and hope into her mother and father's relationship; they had been drifting from one another for some time, like sailboats on a Sargasso Sea of ennui and weariness. Olivia was their Gulf Stream, bringing with her warmer climes and much-needed rejuvenation.

They might even have named her Liv, the Norwegian variant of Olivia. It would have been perfect from an etymological point of view, since the Norwegian noun *liv* means *life*. But her Italian relatives would have struggled with that name. It was too short, not enough syllables and vowels. And there was not enough sing-song in there, either. Olivia was definitely worth singing to the heavens about. She was a godsend, living proof from above that her parents truly did belong together, that they were compatible. Olivia was the hope, the lifeline. Olivia was the olive leaf.

Mother Nature must have a sick sense of irony. Only she could conspire with Destiny to allow a child named Olivia to pass below an olive branch and offer her no hope. Then again, another mother—*my* mother—would often say that life is full of irony and paradox. "'A vita è bella, pure quanno è brutta," she'd say in her beautiful Irpinian dialect. Life is beautiful, even when it's ugly.

The beauty of the olive trees swaying in the afternoon breeze is undeniable, their dusty leaves rustling and crinkling like the whispers of angels. The summer soundscape is intensified by the incessant chirping of crickets, their stridulations a soft backdrop of white noise. The sun sparkles and glistens off the water, ripples forming outward from a single point in the middle of the pool, as if a periscope has just been retracted.

Olivia hears a muffled splash from above, but she barely notices as the tree branch moves farther out of reach and her chest is filled with hot coals. She knows what she wants, but she can no longer ignore what she needs. Her coughs and splutters are not only muffled and silenced by the chlorinated water that engulfs her, but they provide no relief from the burning coals in her lungs. The branch seems to withdraw its hand, its olive-green fingers seeping from the edges of her vision.

Two huge, callous-ridden hands with powerful, vice-like fingers find her extended arms and pull her upward. Olivia is launched out of the water and onto the hard concrete at the edge of the water.

Her eyes are open. But they are blank, glazing over. The whites of those infant eyes are larger than normal. But they communicate nothing: no fear, no anxiety, nothing. She knows what she wants, and she knows what she needs, too: air. But her body is limp, her chest motionless. Her lips blue.

The angels have ceased their whispering. The olive trees have stopped swaying in the afternoon breeze. Even the crickets have muted their chirping, almost as if it were a mark of respect. Mother Nature takes a deep breath, and the silence is ugly, brutal.

CHAPTER 1

The Italian Hillbilly Ideal

I spent the summer of 1979 hanging out with my redneck hillbilly Italian cousins high up in the densely wooded hillsides of Irpinia, in southern Italy.

Now, when I use the terms *hillbilly* and *redneck*, I do it in a purely descriptive manner. My Irpinian cousins were rednecks because they spent long hours working in the sun, so their necks were literally red from sunburn. Sun cream was for pussies . . . and city folk. Same thing, really. Besides, the amount of sweat their bodies produced when they toiled away in the scorching sun—be it on top of some building site scaffolding as casual manual laborers or tilling their own land to produce foodstuffs they could sell at the local market to help make their ragged ends meet—would only wash the sun cream away.

And, I use the word *hillbilly* because, well, they lived in the hills. They also embraced many of the typical hillbilly values that their more famous Appalachian cousins displayed. These values included making do with what you have, working hard, putting food on the table for your wife and kids, keeping yourself to yourself, and making sure you stayed off the government's radar. And it was not difficult to stay off that radar when you considered where these hillbilly cousins of mine lived—an anonymous village called Forino.

Forino is so anonymous that even people who live in Irpinia haven't heard of it. Forino is so unremarkable, in fact, that its Wikipedia entry is the same length as that of Finnish politician Ilmi Hallsten, who served as a member of Finland's parliament from 1919 to 1922. Ever heard of Ilmi Hallsten? Exactly my point!

If you were to draw a fifty-kilometer circle around Forino on a map, you would find many famous places inside that circle— places like Pompeii, Sorrento, Capri, and Amalfi, to mention a few. Hundreds of millions of tourists have visited these places, but none of those tourists will have visited Forino, not even by accident. Forino is less than an hour's drive from Napoli International Airport, but that drive from the terminal building feels like time travel back through the ages.

Forino in the 1970s and '80s, along with much of rural Irpinia, had remained impervious to the advances of modern society. It was as if life there was being played out on a videocassette recorder while the rest of the world was being streamed on Netflix and HBO.

Hillbilly Forino is as anonymous and forgotten as many of its more famous hillbilly counterparts in deepest Kentucky and West Virginia. I've been to these places in the States, and the similarities are more than striking, although I would say that the food in Irpinia is much better.

The hilly, densely forested region of Irpinia is largely unknown to non-Italians. Wine aficionados may have heard of it since the vineyards of Irpinia produce a number of internationally renowned DOCG (Denominazione di Origine Controllata e Garantita) wines, like Greco di Tufo, Taurasi, and Fiano di Avellino.

My cousins loved wine but not those fancy DOCG wines. No, they preferred their own hillbilly variety, which was made from homegrown grapes—nothing added, nothing taken away. The trouble with those DOCG wines was that they were artificial, my cousins assured me. They were genetically modified in perfectly landscaped vineyards with grapes that were impregnated with harmful pesticides. Don't be fooled by appearances, they warned me. It takes more than a fancy label and pretentious packaging to make a good wine.

Like any other redneck hillbilly folk anywhere in the world, these people did not take kindly to unnecessary airs and graces. Salt of the earth, they were, along with a generous helping of tractor oil, cow manure, and alcohol.

At the time, their theory about homemade wine made a lot of sense to me—at least, in theory. In practice, though, it definitely did not. That summer was the first time I got to sample some of their homemade wine. What an experience that turned out to be. To describe its taste as old socks dipped in paint stripper would be doing a disservice to socks! It took all my willpower not to spit that concoction straight out onto the ground, something that would have caused great offense to my cousins. So I manned up and swallowed.

"Mmmm, yes, I see what you mean about it being completely natural!" I said, trying not to wince as the wine tickled and teased at my gag reflex. "Who needs a DOCG certificate and a fancy label?"

My words were met with a consensual murmur of approval from my cousins, not only of my comments but of me as a person. I was one of them now.

My sister Rosa ended up marrying one of them. Not one of the cousins—although that was not unheard of in Irpinia—but another Irpinian hillbilly redneck. His name was Luigi.

Luigi was old school. He was a couple of years younger than me, but his attitudes and sense of tradition and of obligation to family belonged in a Francis Ford Coppola movie. Before he started officially dating my sister, he came to me to ask for my consent. He'd already asked my father and received a yes from him. Now, the right thing to do was to consult Rosa's older brother and eldest son in the family—me. The conversation felt a bit ridiculous, to be honest, even for 1988, when it took place. But just like when I swallowed my cousins' wine, I played along, thanked him for his kind consideration and respect, and gave him my consent.

I'll never forget how happy he looked—and grateful, although he really had no reason to be. After all, in my eyes, my sister was an independent woman, perfectly capable of making her own decisions in life. I often wonder what would have happened if I'd said no. Would he have respected my wishes? Or would we have had a southern Italian version of Romeo and Juliet? What

I do know for sure is that had Luigi not married my sister, this book may never have been written.

Traditions are important to Luigi, as are superstitions. You shouldn't bottle wine when it's windy, he would say; otherwise, your wine will end up with lots of sediment at the bottom. As if *that* makes any difference to the taste of his "vintage." Luigi is not alone in his superstitious beliefs.

When my sister and Luigi were expecting their first child, Luigi was especially careful to clear away any ropes, strings, or cords. A woman should never step over a rope or a hosepipe or anything that resembles a cord of any kind while she is pregnant, he would say; otherwise, the baby might get its umbilical cord wrapped around its own neck.

Or how about this one? A woman should never bottle her tomatoes when she is having her period, because the sauce will end up tasting sour and metallic.

But the most bizarre superstition I heard was when my auntie warned my sister to make sure she put a pair of scissors in her bra on her wedding day. Even Luigi hadn't heard of that one before, so he asked my auntie why. That would protect his bride from any gossiping tongues talking about her, she explained. They wouldn't dare to wag their tongues when they knew the bride had a pair of scissors at hand to cut those wagging tongues off. And sure enough, Rosa had a pair of scissors stuffed down her bra the day she married Luigi.

Luigi is a builder by trade. He can put his hand to just about any job around the home, and, judging by the vast array of tools that litter his underground garage—hammers, screwdrivers, torque wrenches, pipe wrenches, grease guns, compressors, pointing trowels, angle grinders, and even his very own portable concrete mixer—Luigi is your man to call if you need anything fixed or built. Luigi is a regular DIY man, a proper Mr. Fixit.

Like many of his Irpinian compatriots, and contrary to the stereotypical image of an ever-gregarious Italian, Luigi is a quiet, somewhat introverted soul who keeps himself to himself, happiest when he is left in peace to beaver away at some project on his house or on his land. Methodical and focused, he is a man who takes exceptional pride in his work, no matter how large or small the task may be.

By far the largest task he ever undertook was the construction of his own family home, which he accomplished pretty much on his own and by hand. You would have to search far to find a prouder man than Luigi as he told you stories about how he had a hand in laying down every single brick and every sliver of cement.

The house he and my sister live in is by no means the biggest or the grandest in the area—that honor probably goes to the local mafia boss (yes, they do exist in real life)—but it certainly is one of the prettiest, with its dark wooden shutters, shady porticos and pergolas, half-circle terracotta roof tiles, and terraced garden. However, to say that the house has been designed or landscaped would be an exaggeration, as well as an aberration of hillbilly values; being chic or *en vogue* was not one of them.

What *is* an important hillbilly value is being self-sufficient. A loan from the bank is a no-no, unless absolutely necessary. Besides, getting a loan puts you on the government radar. You only buy what you can afford, what you can pay for yourself—and preferably in cash. Even to this day, Luigi still does not have a credit card! Neither does my father, for that matter. Where most people take up a loan with the bank to buy a home, Luigi financed it himself, with his own money—cash, of course.

Since it would have taken far too long to save up enough cash to build the entire home in one go, he built different parts of the house as and when he'd accumulated enough money. This meant that his house went up in stages—lots of stages. The foundations went in first, followed by a new floor, a set of windows, then a set of shutters to cover the windows. Next was the adjoining staircase, then the drainpipes, and so on, until the house was habitable and ready to move into. It probably took Luigi a decade to complete all the stages and all the floors, but he managed to do it. And he did it with great resilience, grit, and creativity. Or, as Luigi would put it in one of his many typically Irpinian aphorisms, "U 'talian se fa sicc', ma nun mor!" (An Italian might get skinny, but he doesn't die!) And when Luigi used the word *Italian*, he meant *southern* Italian—an Irpinian Italian.

The result of this way of building has given Luigi's house a whimsical air, a kind of make-it-up-as-you-go-along feel. The house doesn't have so much as a *je ne sais quoi* about it, as a *je m'en fous*. There's a faux wishing well in this corner of the garden, a mini wooden windmill in that corner, over there by the two hollowed-out-tree-trunk flowerpots, and a miniature shrine over in the corner by the fake fountain. And then there is the hand-engraved wooden plaque above the entrance, which is suspended on a couple of chains that I suspect were originally tethered to a couple of bath plugs.

This ingenious sign bears the name of the house: Rose Cottage. What a gesture! After a decade of backbreaking labor, Luigi named the house after his wife, my sister, Rosa.

As if that weren't enough, to the side of the house is Luigi's *pièce de résistance*: the mosaic beneath the olive tree where my sister often sits to enjoy a coffee in the early spring sun. Well, when I say mosaic, it's more like a motley montage of masonry debris, floor tiles, and flat-sided rocks that Luigi da Vinci has set into a four-inch-thick concrete floor. The entire mosaic provides a framework, a picture frame for the most important part of the entire masterpiece: a group of white stones that spell out the word *ROSA*.

Every time I see that sign above the entrance and the mosaic under that olive tree, I say to myself, "Wow, these two are in it for the long haul." Every time Olivia sees that *mo-say-ick*, she asks if Luigi can write *her* name in the cement too. That has never happened, but we did christen her Olivia Rosa Riccardi. Her godparents, naturally, are Rosa and Luigi.

Luigi and Rosa's house has been my preferred holiday location ever since they moved in with their toddler sons in the mid-1990s. Every year I go back there, Luigi has added something new to the house or to the garden: a new path, a new gate, a new bench to sit on, a pair of swans to flank the entrance into the olive grove.

When you explore the house, it is clear that Luigi has a particular liking for one type of building material—stone. He's used stone walls, stone paths, stone floors. Whenever Luigi takes an afternoon nap, he most likely does so on one of his stone walls or benches, even when there is a perfectly good sun lounger or chair right next to him.

Years of dedicated, heavy labor with his stones have left their mark on Luigi's body. These days, he often complains about searing pain down his neck and spine, even though his bulging shoulder and upper back muscles seem powerful enough to bear the weight of a grizzly. Meanwhile, his hands are riddled with scars and calluses, which you would feel if you were ever to shake his hand. What you would also feel would be the force of his powerful, vice-like fingers. Those fingers have clasped at and lifted countless blocks of granite and limestone with the ease of an industrial crane equipped with giant tongs. Luigi's fingers are so powerful that I am sure they have biceps!

Luigi doesn't use Facebook or Instagram to humblebrag like the rest of us. He doesn't even have internet. Instead, he has his house.

"You know how much a house like this would be worth if I sold it up north?"

It is a question Luigi asks me every time I visit my sister. The question normally surfaces after dinner, after he's had a few glasses of wine—homemade wine, of course. It takes more than a fancy label and pretentious packaging to make a good wine, Luigi proclaims, as if he's been indoctrinated with the same redneck creed as my cousins.

"No idea, Luigi, how much would this house be worth up north?"

"Go on, give me a number. Any number!" Luigi demands.

"A hundred million euro?" I offer, half humoring him, half teasing him because I already know where this conversation is going.

"Okay, okay, make fun if you like, Pellegrino, but even if it *were* a hundred million euro, I still wouldn't sell it. And you know why?"

Yes, I do know why. He told me the year before and the year before that and the year before that too.

"Because I made this house with my own hands. With my own sweat, blood, and tears. For my family. For your sister! And you can't put a price on that!"

And with that, he clasps the bottle of wine with his huge, callous-ridden, crane-claw hands and takes another gulp of his homemade wine.

CHAPTER 2

Whispering Angels and Wandering Witches

My mother used to tell me that if ever something terrible was about to happen, an angel would whisper in your ear.

"There are always whispers of warning," she used to say. "You just need to be listening. That's why you need to pray to the angels every night before you go to sleep."

I remember the first time she said that and how I'd smirked at her.

"Oh, don't be ridiculous, Mamma. I think I'm a bit too old to be praying to angels now."

My reply had the cockiness of a fifteen-year-old boy who thinks that because he's been educated at a fancy grammar school in England, where subjects like Latin and Greek are on the syllabus, he knows a thing or two about life.

"You can smirk all you like," my mother replied. "I may not have an education like you do, but education is much more than just reading and writing, you know. In Italian, *educazione* means both school and upbringing. And you, my boy, are not finished with either one yet."

She wasn't angry at me. At least not visibly so. But she was firm and resolute, putting me in my place in a way that made me feel castigated but still loved. My mother was always good at striking that balance, even when she was having to deal with a self-important grammar school know-it-all like me.

She didn't need reminding that she'd had no formal education. As a child growing up in postwar Italy in the 1940s, there was as little school on the menu as there was food and shelter. Besides, when did schooling become more important than a proper upbringing? Wasn't it Mark Twain who once said, "I never let my schooling interfere with my education"?

"So, have you ever heard an angel whisper in your ear?" I asked my mother.

"Oh, sure," she replied.

"When was the last time you heard it?"

"In a church in England in 1961. I was standing next to your father at the time. I was about to say 'I do' to him!"

"What did the angel whisper to you, Mamma?"

"'Don't do it!'" she cried.

We both fell into a heap of laughter.

"I guess you didn't listen to the angel then, Mamma."

"I guess not. But if I had listened to my angel, I wouldn't have had you, now would I? Or your sister or your little brother. 'A vita è bella, pure quanno è brutta." Life is beautiful, even when it's ugly.

"That makes no sense, Mamma. How can life be beautiful and ugly at the same time?"

"One day you'll understand, Pelli. One day, when you've had some more *educazione*."

My mother often used a shortened version of my name rather than my full name, *Pellegrino*. I had been rechristened Pell by my English friends. All my English friends had shortened versions of their names; that's part of growing up in the UK. Christopher became Chris. Catherine was Cathy or Kate. Roberto was Rob. And Pellegrino became Pell.

My mother thought Pell sounded a bit blunt, though. It lacked that Italian singsong playfulness that Italian names often had. It definitely lacked a vowel at the end. And besides, it needed at least another syllable, preferably with a vowel tagged on to the end of it. *Definitely* more vowels. *Pelliano. Pelliuccio. Pelligno.* Any of those would have been better than the one she came up with in the end: *Pelli.*

The only problem was that she never told me about her choice. At least, not before she'd actually used it for the first time. Had she told me that she wanted to call me Pelli from that moment on, I would have shut her suggestion down, banned her from using it. But the name was invented on the spot, on a whim, a linguistic reflex of euphoria and excitement as she watched me score the winning goal for the Under-10s school football team.

There I was, surrounded by my teammates, basking in the glory of my perfectly placed last-minute winner, a side-footed shot from just outside the six-yard box, when I heard from the touchline the unmistakable cry of an Italian immigrant mother's heavily accented voice, "Well-a done! Bravo, Pelli!"

This was definitely not a good moment for me. My teammates pounced on her words like a pack of hyenas.

"Did your mum just call you *Pelli?*"

"Eh, no, I don't think so," I answered, placing the ball back on the center spot and trying to distract everyone's attention by shouting, "Come on, lads! Let's get another goal!"

"Yes, she did. She just called you *Pelli!*"

"No, she meant to say *Pelé*, not *Pelli*," I replied loudly enough for most of my teammates to hear.

It probably was Pelé she meant to call me. After all, this was the 1970s, a decade that was dominated by Brazilian football, their star player being none other than the one and only Edson Arantes do Nascimento, better known as Pelé. Pelé was on TV and in the newspapers. People talked about him at work, at school, everywhere. And it would have been fine if she had actually called me Pelé. But my mother had an amazing ability to ever so slightly mispronounce foreign words.

She would say things like, "I am popping down to the shop to buy some veggie-*tables*" instead of *veg*etables. My sister and I would tease her by asking her to pick up some meat-*tables* too, and fruit-*tables*, and while she was at it, a dining room-*table* or a billiard-*table* would be good too. She didn't understand that wordplay at all.

Another time, she came back from the shop and told us that

the supermarket had had lots of special offers that day, including potatoes, which were very *chip*.

"Chip, Mamma?"

"Yes, *chip*—you know, no cost a lot-a money. *Chip*."

"But, Mamma, these aren't chips," I said as I peeked into her shopping bag. "These are potatoes, and you haven't even peeled them yet, so they can't be chips!"

"Chip, not chip. You know, chip, the opposite of expensive," she protested.

"Cheeeeep, Mamma. You have to make the word longer," I tried to explain in a way she would understand, since I knew that Italian didn't distinguish between long and short vowel sounds like English. In English, this can mean the difference between saying *ship* or *sheep*. *Shin* or *sheen*. Or *shit* or *sheet*. You must have heard the one about the Italian tourist staying at an English hotel who asked the room service personnel if he could have a nice shit on the bed.

"Oh, you kids drive-a me crazy!" she answered, exasperated. "I wish you would-a just leave-a me alone and-a give me some-a *piss* and quiet."

So, thanks to yet another of my mother's mispronunciations, Pelli became my new name for the rest of that football season. I had to take endless teasing from my friends about my new nickname: Smelly Pelli, Pelli-copter, Pelli with the big fat belly, Pelli the Elephant packed his trunk and said goodbye to the circus, and many, many more varieties of Pelli.

It was a relief that was my last year of primary school, because it wasn't until I started my new secondary school with new classmates that I could wipe the slate clean and go back to Pell. It took me a little longer to persuade my mother to drop Pelli. I was perhaps one of the few people in the world who welcomed Pelé's retirement from the football stage in 1977.

But one thing my mother never stopped doing was believing in angels. And witches—especially witches, in fact. Why, you could see witches wandering around the neighborhood at night, she would tell me, although she would also assure me that they were sad witches, not bad ones. Most of my family in Italy believed in witches too. Luigi certainly did, although I always figured that in Luigi's case, it was as much down to his fondness for a certain southern Italian liqueur called Strega as anything else.

Strega—the name means *witch* in Italian—is a potent Italian herbal liqueur made from over seventy exotic ingredients, such as Ceylon cinnamon, Florentine iris, Samnite mint, and the all-important saffron. It's the saffron that gives Strega its distinctive bright yellow hue and makes it stand out as the natural centerpiece of many a drinks cabinet south of Rome.

North of Rome, you'll usually find another yellow liqueur called Galliano. But in the south, it's always Strega. Because Strega originates from the south, from the Irpinian town of Benevento.

Benevento lies just fifty kilometers from Forino. When you drive those fifty kilometers, you pass many fantastic DOCG vineyards and wine distilleries. You also pass by plenty of hillbilly villages just like Forino, where most people will be turning their noses up at fancy labels and packaging.

But there's one label that southerners will never consider too fancy, and that is the Strega label, with its distinctive crimson red logo emblazoned across a bright yellow background, and an image of witches dancing around a walnut tree. Why witches? Because even before the first bottle of Strega was sold in 1860, Benevento had already become famous for its witches.

For me, a bottle of Strega reminds me of Christmases in England. Every Christmas, we would "do the rounds," as my parents called it. We would visit our fellow Italian immigrant friends and family and wish them a happy Christmas.

At each house we went to, we would be offered a selection of sweets and cakes. The sweets came in the form of typically southern Italian white sugar-coated almonds called *confetti alla mandorla*. The cake was called panettone, the famous cupola-shaped Italian fruitcake, which not only tasted delicious but also had an important practical function—to soak up the vast amounts of liqueur the adults would drink at each port of call.

There were lots of different types of liqueurs to choose from, too. First there was brandy, usually Vecchia Romagna or Stock 84. Then there were the vermouths and aperitifs, like Cinzano, Martini, Amaretto Di Saronno, and an odd drink called Cynar, which was made from artichokes.

I could never understand how anyone could come up with the idea of making a liqueur out of artichokes. The idea of drinking it was even more bizarre. No doubt, people would drink it with the same unflappable conviction with which they drank each other's homemade wine.

Sometimes you would be offered something sparkling. Never champagne, though. That was too expensive for most immigrant Italian communities. And besides, it was French! Instead, the bubbles came in the form of sparkling wines like Asti Spumante or, if you were really splashing out, a Prosecco. And finally, the *pièce de résistance*, the Strega.

Christmas was one of the few days in the year that my mother would drink Strega. I could smell it on her breath for the rest of the day.

While sightings of witches were quite common, the chances of spotting an angel meandering around the neighborhood or prancing around a walnut tree were slim. But you could hear them. Oh, yes, people like Luigi had no doubts that angels whispered in our ears all the time, especially when there was impending danger of some sort. The question was not whether the angels spoke but whether the people they whispered to were actually listening to them.

I certainly didn't hear the angels on that summer's day as my daughter took her first step into the pool. I think about Olivia's periscope arms reaching for that olive branch, and I know I should have been there next to her. I know that now. But I wasn't. I was in the kitchen.

. . .

I blame it on the garlic! A whiff of garlic from our summer rental home kitchen as it began sizzling in the pan was all it took to lure me away from the pool. My sister and Luigi were there too.

The house we'd rented was only a couple of hours from Forino by car, and there was a spare bedroom for them, so they'd made an on-the-spot decision, flung some clothes into a travel bag, and headed for Puglia.

As the two of them lay there sunbathing by the pool, neither of them was especially lured by the garlic, their noses already desensitized by years of daily exposure to Italian cuisine. The only thing they were being lured toward was sleep, aided by the gentle rippling of water against the pool's edge and the persistent chirping of crickets in the olive groves around them.

Luigi had found himself a customary spot to enjoy his slumber on top of a small limestone parapet. Just as if he were at home in his own garden, he preferred to feel the rough texture of stone on his body to the more conventional materials of a sunbed or a deck chair. As he lay on his masonry bed, facedown, you could almost hear his red neck and broad shoulders begin to sizzle like pancetta in a pan. Judging from the light snore that could already be heard above the ripples of the pool, he was absolutely fine with that.

I can still smell the garlic in my nostrils today. I can taste it on the back of my tongue. Every time someone puts garlic into the spluttering olive oil of a saucepan, I am thrust back into that kitchen, where my senses were being bombarded with the smells and sounds of Italy. It was a sensory hijacking of my prefrontal cortex, conspiring against my rational self. If that sound and that smell can persuade fifty million or so tourists a year to part with their holiday money, what chance did I have of resisting it? What chance does a whispering angel have against such a sensory overload?

And why the hell would angels *whisper* in your ear, anyway? If they are there to warn of impending danger, shouldn't they be screaming? Shouldn't they be blowing into a long clarion or something? Renaissance paintings are full of angels blowing trumpets. There are two of them perched on top of the Italian Constitutional Courthouse in Rome, clarions in hand, trumpeting away. None of them are whispering. Perhaps then I could have heard their warnings.

Of course, it didn't help that we had rented a particular type of house for that year's summer holiday, one that is both typical and unique to the region of Italy we were staying in.

Puglia is the heel of Italy, often called the Caribbean of Italy or the Maldives of Italy because of its white sandy beaches and crystal-clear turquoise waters. Puglia is also where you will find a type of house called a *trullo*.

Trullo houses—or *trulli*, to use the Italian plural form—are wonderful buildings. They are traditional dry-stone huts with circular-shaped rooms and conical roofs. Since each room has its own individual conical roof, a trullo house with three or more rooms resembles a miniature fairy-tale house. A trullo is the kind of place where an Italian troll would want to live. A *trollo* in a *trullo*.

Trulli first appeared on the Puglia landscape in the fourteenth century. What they all had in common when they were built was that their walls and roofs were of dry-stone construction. No cement was ever used in their construction. And there was a good reason for this. A good *Italian* reason.

Like any other European country, Italy had property taxes for private homes. Income tax is relatively easy to avoid, since it is easy to hide one's income, especially when that income comes in the form of notes and coins. Homes, on the other hand, are much more difficult—if not impossible—to hide. Or are they? What if your home is a dry-stone construction? What if you could dismantle your home at the drop of a hat just before the tax inspector visited your property? After all, tax inspectors back in the day came on horseback, which would give you enough time to do just that.

By the time the inspector arrived, that house could have been transformed into a wall, or a stable, or a sheep pen, none of which are homes. No house, no tax. And when the tax inspector left, it didn't take long to reassemble the walls and roof of your house again. It was Italian anti-authority ingenuity at its best.

Today, of course, the inspectors no longer take hours or days to arrive on horseback. Everything has been documented and catalogued in some digital file somewhere, while satellites have photographed practically every building on the planet. This is why the modern-day *trullo* no longer uses a dry-stone construction. Instead, the more-than-one-meter-thick limestone walls have been rendered and whitewashed with cement and paint. This acts as an effective form of insulation against the scorching Puglia heat outside, a natural air-conditioning system that also happens to be ecofriendly.

The heavy limestone brickwork also acts as a highly effective form of soundproofing. It is so effective, in fact, that not even the clarion call of a host of hollering angels could have penetrated it.

But who am I kidding? I can't blame the walls of a house for my parental negligence—or the smell of sizzling garlic—for the fact that I should never have left a three-year-old alone by the pool. It's this undeniable, painful truth that I am doomed to carry around with me for the rest of my life, a sense of guilt and shame that I failed to protect my daughter, that I gave precedence to the gentle sizzling of garlic over the whispering of angels.

CHAPTER 3

Cars, Cruelty, and *la Bella Figura*

My father let me drive his car for the first time when I was nine years old. Yes, nine! Okay, so my father sat right next to me, and he was responsible for changing gears, and we *were* driving in an empty cow field in the English countryside, but still.

I remember we'd stopped there for a family picnic, and after a couple of glasses of his homemade wine, my father asked me if I wanted to drive his new car. Well, when I say new, I mean, new to *him*. It was a 1971 brown Hillman Hunter that he'd picked up secondhand. It only had thirty thousand miles on the clock, which was nothing for a three-year-old car, he assured me.

"Drive it?" I asked, somewhat incredulously. "Me? But I am not even ten years old yet."

"That's all right," he beamed back in his native Irpinia dialect. "But don't worry. I'll be sitting right next to you."

"What about if the police see us?" I asked, still trying to work out if he was serious about this.

"What police?" he said, shrugging his shoulders in that iconic gesture of feigned innocence that so many Italian football players have used during a game when they are about to be booked for a serious foul.

He gulped down the last of his homemade wine and snorted again, "What fucking police?"

. . .

There was always so much violence and disdain in my father's voice, as if he bore a constant grudge against a world that had dealt him such a bad hand. As the son of an immigrant growing up in the UK, I could never quite understand that mentality. I mean, had he not been given one of life's golden tickets by being allowed to move to a new country and start afresh? A place where there were almost limitless opportunities for work—albeit cheap manual labor, but still—and where his children could grow up with the very things he had been deprived of, like free education and free health care?

I remember this one time we were visiting a local Irpinian monastery on one of our trips back to the homeland, a place called the Sanctuary of San Gerardo of Maiella. My father believed that a donation to the monastery in his name would somehow bring celestial blessings on his family and alter the cards that he had been dealt in life, so he would return to the monastery every time he was back home. I guess on this one occasion, his patience was starting to run thin. It didn't help that the queue for donations that day seemed especially long. Either the donation system worked and so people were coming back for more, or Catholics were even more gullible than I thought.

When we finally made it to the window marked *Offerte* (Donations), we were met by a rather tired-looking elderly monk with a hearing aid who sat behind tempered glass so thick that it looked more like the window of a corporate bank than a monastery. My father slid a large banknote underneath the windowpane and watched as the monk quickly whipped it out of sight into a drawer under his desk. Once his money was secure, the monk glanced up in a disinterested manner, his pen hovering above a thick tome of names and addresses, ready to take my father's details.

"The Lord blesses you and your family for your generous donation," the monk said, sounding more like a robot than a genuinely appreciative member of the cloth. "And in whose name should I make this donation?" he added.

"Famiglia Riccardi da Forino, Santo Padre," replied my father. The Riccardi family from Forino.

Strictly speaking, the title *Santo Padre* was reserved for the Pope, but the robot monk either didn't hear my father's mistaken form of address or didn't consider it sacrilegious enough to correct him.

The monk began to enter the details into his book, reading out loud as he slowly wrote the words: "Riccardi . . . family . . . froooom . . . Torino."

At least we now knew why the queue was so long.

"Eh, excuse me, Santo Padre," my father interrupted. "It's Forino, not Torino."

"Torino?" the monk asked.

"No. Forino," my father replied, trying his best to remain patient and respectful of a man of the cloth.

"Torino, with a T?" the monk asked again.

"No, Forino with an F," my father replied. I could sense the pressure building up inside him.

"Ah, Forino . . . with an F," the monk replied. "F, as in Firenze!"

"Yes, Santo Padre, F as in Firenze," my father offered with fake cheeriness, before muttering under his breath, "Or F as in fucking deaf twat!"

That was the last year my father went to the Sanctuary of San Gerardo of Maiella.

. . .

Sure enough, five minutes later, I was driving my father's 1971 Hillman Hunter around an English cow field, straining my neck to peer over the steering wheel, my boyish grins punctuated only by my father's instructions to press and release the clutch while he engaged the gears for me. Although I mainly just drove around in aimless circles, leaving behind a distinct trail of mashed dandelions and squashed cowpats, I distinctly recall how powerful it felt to be propelling a clump of metal forward with such ease, simply by pressing a pedal under my foot.

It was also one of the few times I actually felt close to my father, and safe with him by my side.

. . .

While I was busy philosophizing over Latin classical prose in my upscale English grammar school, most of my male cousins weren't even attending school anymore. They had all opted out of school so that they could start working and contributing to the family's all too often empty coffers. For them, food for thought came second to food on the table. Among the thick forests of the Irpinia mountains, I learned a few lessons about what being a man meant in that part of the world. Far away from the prying eyes of government regulation officers and child welfare services, these cousins of mine worked hard and played hard in ways I could never have gotten away with back home in England.

For example, they all drove cars before they were legally allowed to drive. During the summer of '79, when I was just fourteen years old, I drove a car on my own for the very first time. Driving a car on your own for the first time is usually a memorable experience; there's something about indulging in the forbidden that makes it all the more exciting and irresistible. Just ask Adam and Eve.

Safety was the last thing on anybody's mind as my cousins in Irpinia showed me how to do wheel spins and handbrake turns and then handed the car over to me. There was no passenger to change gears for me now, no safety net—just me, man and machine.

"What if the police see us?" I asked them.

"What police?" they jeered back at me, each one of them making the same body and facial expressions of an Italian footballer who's just been given a yellow card. "What fucking police?"

Another important lesson I learned with my hillbilly cousins was that seat belts were for wimps. For both drivers *and* passengers. I remember one day we were about to set off on a little road trip. The eldest of the cousins, Ninuccio, was driving. There were six of us in the car, even though the vehicle had only five seats. Four boisterous teenagers noisily squished themselves into the back bench of the car. As the visiting guest of honor, I was given the front passenger seat, right next to the driver.

Instinctively, I buckled up my seat belt with a loud click. *Clunk-click*, every trip, that's what the British TV adverts of the seventies taught us. A heavy silence filled the car.

Ninuccio turned to me, looked me straight in the eyes, and asked, "What are you doing? Don't you trust my driving?"

What else could I do except apologize and unbuckle my seat belt?

· · ·

If there is one thing you never do in that part of the world, it's challenge or question another man's driving skills. Or any skills, come to think of it. And certainly not in front of his peers. One of the most important forms of social capital a man can have in places like Irpinia—and Appalachia, for that matter—is their honor. This is especially the case when they have so little capital of any other kind at their disposal, be it material wealth, education, or business achievements. This is why so-called honor cultures are often found in the most poverty-stricken or underprivileged areas of the world. Often, all they have of any worth is their honor.

In Italy, they call it *la bella figura*: "the beautiful impression." *Bella figura* is the need to create a good impression to the outside world. At its worst, *bella figura* manifests itself as an overemphasis on superficial appearances, like the clothes you wear, the car you drive, the house you live in. At its best, though, *bella figura* urges people to create a positive picture *even when* their resources are limited.

The most common way my family did this was to provide magnificent levels of hospitality, especially hospitality of the culinary kind. That's why, whenever we were invited to someone's house for dinner in Irpinia, they would lavish us with excessive amounts of food.

By doing this, they are communicating two main messages: First, we greatly value and respect you as our guests. Second, even though we are underprivileged, we still have enough money and resources to provide you with a feast fit for royalty. This is how *la bella figura* is preserved.

Stinginess is extremely frowned on, even if you are not well off. I once shared a house with three other men in Leeds while I was studying at the university there. As was the norm in those days, we all shared common expenses, like gas, electricity, and food. One morning, I was having a lie-in after a particularly heavy late night out, and I heard a knock on my door. It was one of my housemates. Let's call him Neil.

"Good morning, Pell," Neil said hesitantly, the look on my hungover face obviously communicating to him that I did not appreciate an early morning wake-up call the day after a student party. "Err, sorry to wake you up, but . . ."

"What the fuck, Neil? It's eight o'clock in the morning. I'm trying to sleep."

"Yes, err, I know. Sorry again. It's just . . . it's just that I bought a box of matches for the gas fire."

This was the winter of 1986. Gas fires in student houses could only be ignited by turning a knob to release the gas and then lighting it with a naked flame. As you can imagine, there were an awful lot of emergency calls to the fire service from student residences in the 1980s.

"And?" I inquired, completely mystified as to where this early morning conversation was going.

"Well, I just wanted to say," continued Neil hesitantly, "that the matches cost 20 pence."

Twenty pence in 1986 is the equivalent of about 50 pence today (half a British pound)—half a euro, or just over 60 US cents. Peanuts, to use a universal international currency.

"And?" I asked, sensing now where this was going but refusing to believe that we were actually going there.

"Well," continued Neil, "if you could just leave your share on the kitchen table downstairs, that would be lovely. Thanks." And off he went to class as if what he'd just done was the most normal and accepted behavior known to man.

I couldn't believe that Neil had actually woken me up from my hangover to ask for the grand sum of 5 pence! 5p! Suffice it to say, Neil did *not* create a *bella figura* that day. And I was sure to take out exactly one quarter of the matchbox's contents—twenty-one matches to be precise—that I then kept in my room as a constant reminder of how *not* to behave if one wants to uphold *la bella figura*.

Neil wouldn't have lasted long among the rednecks of Irpinia, I can tell you, where honor cultures, with all their mechanisms of social interaction are very much alive and kicking even today.

. . .

I learned quickly that if I wanted to be accepted among my male peers, I had to be a tough, fearless, and sometimes even reckless man. Driving without a license and without a seat belt was indeed reckless and irresponsible. It was also wildly liberating and enormously gratifying—like the time I learned how to use a shotgun.

"Haven't you ever fired a gun?" Ninuccio exclaimed incredulously one day.

Implied in his words was the notion that you simply couldn't call yourself a real man unless you'd fired a gun. All of my male cousins had weapons. Ninuccio had two or three. One he kept in the trunk of his car—just in case.

"Just in case of what?" I asked him once.

"Just in case we come across a wolf."

"You know that the name Irpinia comes from the old Latin word *hirpus*, which means wolf? That's why Avellino football club's nickname is the Wolves and why they have the emblem of a wolf on their shirts."

"And?" Ninuccio replied, evidently unimpressed by my erudite, grammar-school insight.

"Well, wolves are part of Irpinia's history and heritage. I wouldn't be surprised if they are a protected species around here."

"All I know is that wolves attack and eat my livestock!"

"Yeah, I guess you have a point," I said, suddenly acutely aware that I had touched a nerve with Ninuccio.

Here I was, an out-of-town urban tourist lecturing the locals about matters I couldn't possibly understand, casting aspersions on his way of life, trying to intimidate him with my etymological expertise, using fancy words like *heritage*. It was a good job I hadn't said this in front of the other cousins.

In actual fact, it was quite unusual to spot a wolf. They are far too timid as animals. Besides, most of them had been frightened off by shotgun brandishing Irpinian hillbillies. What Ninuccio called wolves were usually not wolves at all, though, but wild dogs.

One evening, he suggested we take a drive with his friends. My inquiry as to where we were heading was met with enigmatic silence and a wry smile. As we cruised around the Forino hillsides, I noticed Ninuccio seemed to be scoping the surroundings. Now and again, he would slow down, roll down his window, and peer into the thick bushes that lined the narrow road.

"What are you looking for?" I asked.

"Nothing," he replied.

Just then, a black-and-white mongrel skipped out from behind the bushes, its inquisitive eyes sparkling in Ninuccio's car headlights. The dog seemed strangely unafraid of us. Inquisitively, the mutt cocked its head and wagged its tail at us, as if to ask what we were doing up there in the mountain so late in the day.

Ninuccio calmly and purposefully got out of the car and made his way toward the trunk, opened it, and took out his 12-gauge. He then proceeded to casually walk directly toward the dog with the demeanor of a man who is about to offer his own dog a snack or a pat on the head. However, Ninuccio had neither food nor praise for this creature. What he did have was a shotgun and a bad attitude toward any potential predator of his precious livestock.

His weapon hung down by his side, parallel with his right leg, in the blind side of the dog's field of view. I didn't even see him raise the shotgun to his shoulder. All I heard was the sharp crack of the firearm as it was fired, followed a microsecond later by a low thwack of the steel pellets on the dog's torso.

The animal hit the asphalt instantly. No movement. No dramatic, drawn-out death scene like they have in Hollywood movies. That's not how animals—or people, for that matter—die, at least not when the bullet hits the right place. It's the same with drowning. In Hollywood, people drown shouting and screaming, their arms flailing desperately in the air. In reality, people drown quietly. Very quietly.

The sparkling eyes of that black-and-white mongrel were sparkling no more. Ninuccio turned around, put the shotgun in the trunk again, and we drove off.

I wanted to scream, but I didn't say a word. I wanted to scream at him for shooting a defenseless animal. And I wanted to cry tears of empathic pain and sorrow for that poor dog. But I didn't. I kept my true feelings inside. If I'd shown my true feelings in that moment, it would have been seen as a direct rejection and affront to their values, to their way of living. Who was I to tell them how to live their lives? I was nothing more than an urban tourist—city folk, a pussy. But most of all, if I'd displayed those feelings of pain and sorrow in front of my male peers, they would have seen it as a sign of weakness. The instruction manual on how to be a real man was different in those days, especially in the hillbilly south of Italy.

I guess it was safe to say that, in the space of a couple of months in that summer of 1979, I felt that I had come of age. I had lost much of my childhood innocence and gained a few extra pounds of cockiness. I no longer believed in Father Christmas, and I certainly didn't believe in angels.

CHAPTER 4

Preikestolen

Where are those angels now? I think as I peer over the edge of the cliff and down at the frigid water below. I am standing on the Pulpit Rock, or *Preikestolen*, to give it its Norwegian name, a square slab of granite formed over ten thousand years ago during the last ice age. I'm now sometime in the future. I'm not sure when. In fact, it doesn't matter when. All I know is that it is after our holiday in Puglia, when time and space have become a bit blurry. This could be real, or I could be dreaming. It doesn't really matter. They say that the brain can't tell the difference anyway. If it is a dream, then I know why my subconscious chose Preikestolen. It's a place I fell in love with the first time I ever came here. I'm sure others have done the same. Tom Cruise was so smitten by Preikestolen that he used it for the final action sequence of his *Mission: Impossible—Fallout* movie. In the film, the action takes place in Kashmir, but you only need to have been to Preikestolen once to know that scene was not filmed in Kashmir at all.

Preikestolen juts from the fjord cliff face, straight out into midair like a preacher's pulpit in a church—hence its name—suspended 604 meters above the icy waters of Lysefjord below. One of Norway's top tourist attractions, the site offers both stunning panoramas and relatively easy access. Greeting tourists at the end of the two-hour hike to the top of Preikestolen is a place of stunning natural beauty, a place where they feel at one with Mother Nature and at the same time at her mercy. That precarious and fragile balance is what makes this place so fascinating.

As if to accentuate this dichotomy, there are no fences or safety ropes of any kind between the tourist and the void below. For Norwegians, this is in line with their national mindset of keeping the country's pristine natural surroundings as untouched and unspoiled by human intervention as possible. If Preikestolen had been in Germany or the United States, I am pretty sure they would have erected a fence around the edges of the cliff top. Maybe even an electric one—just in case.

Had Preikestolen been in Irpinia, they would have constructed a fence just short of the actual viewpoint and charged you an entrance fee like they do on Vesuvius. All major credit cards *not* accepted, naturally. And when you made it to the top, someone would greet you with a glass of some local DOCG wine, although you shouldn't be surprised if that particular vintage had a distinctly sock-like aftertaste.

One small step in the wrong direction, one small gust of wind, one slip of the foot, one whiff of garlic sizzling in a pan, and life changes irreversibly.

"At one with Mother Nature and at her mercy," I mumble to myself.

Standing on the edge of this precipice, I realize that all that lies between me and a certain fate is an endless supply of some of the purest and most life-giving air in the world. This air is so pure, in fact, that city folk in China are actually paying entrepreneurial Norwegians extortionate amounts of money to have it bottled up and transported to their smog-ridden cities, where they can inhale it into their clogged-up lungs.

Another one of Mother Nature's cruel ironies, I think as I envision myself flying through luxurious life-giving air toward a certain end.

Standing on the edge of this scarred granite tabletop cliff edge, I feel alive and dangerously vulnerable at the same time. As I inch my toes over the cliff edge and stare downward into the abyss, I am overwhelmed by an irresistible urge to jump. Eighteen seconds. That's all it would take to fall 604 meters.

I read that once in a magazine article about BASE jumping. These dicers with death travel from all over the world to come to this particular fjord to get their eighteen seconds of adrenaline: eighteen seconds of free fall for my life to flash before my eyes. Would I regret my decision on the way down? If I did, it would only be for eighteen seconds. After that, no more shame. No more guilt. I take a deep breath, filling my lungs with air that Beijing citizens can only dream of.

'A vita è bella, pure quanno è brutta, I think. Is this what my mother meant when she said those words? The ugliness of the

situation I am in right now is framed in the unparalleled beauty of a Norwegian fjord.

For an instant, my center of gravity shifts forward, then back again, swaying like the heavy pendulum of a grandfather clock. The tipping point is millimeters away. One more nudge, and it's done.

I suddenly recoil back, my heart racing. What the fuck am I thinking? What am I *doing?* I glance around to see if any of the other hikers have noticed me, if anyone has read my thoughts, if anyone has seen the shame emblazoned on my chest, if anyone heard an angel whisper in *their* ear. But people are too absorbed with their selfies and Instagram posts to notice.

I back away from the edge and head for the safety of a grassy knoll on the mountainside. A wave of angst and shame floods my body. I feel angst at the real peril I'd been in just seconds ago and shame that I would even consider such an ultimate act of egoism. The shame I will need to deal with later. Right now, the constricting pain in my chest is my most immediate concern.

Angst or angina? It must be angst. Angina is much more serious. Physiologically, they are two quite different conditions. Etymologically, they are the same: constriction, narrowing, tightness. The etymology helps explain why so many Norwegian towns like Stavanger, Geiranger, Levanger, Høyanger, Varanger, Orkanger, Bremanger, Fjøsanger, and Kaupanger are situated where they are—at the end of tight, narrow, constricting fjords, often with high surrounding cliffs and mountains that add to the sense of claustrophobia and constriction of their location. Places of anguish, perhaps? The Norwegian word for "regret"—*anger*—has the same origin as angst and angina.

This would be the perfect place to jump with regret, with anguish. To jump, to smash loudly through the waterline, and then to drown quietly. Eighteen seconds of constricting, suffocating regret for all the things I wish I hadn't done, all the things I wish I *had* done, all the things that you are about to read about.

I was so close. I actually felt the magnetic pull of my soul toward that fatal tipping point when free will and control give way to gravity. A psychiatrist once explained to me that that very same magnetic tug was a person's best defense mechanism *against* jumping off a building or a cliff edge. He told me that you *should* walk toward the edge, and you *should* feel the urge to jump, because that will lead to the appropriate amount of fear and panic that will help force you to back away from such a life-threatening place. It's when you *don't* get scared or when you *don't* get that feeling of angst that you should be worried, because that's when your neurological sensors no longer understand the danger.

If only that same neurological safety mechanism applied to water. I know that Olivia felt no such tug of panic and fear when she first stepped over the edge of the pool and made her way down the steps toward that *mo-say-ick* below the silky waterline. How long can a three-year-old hold her breath—longer than eighteen seconds? At least she would have been too young to fully appreciate such complex emotional states as angst and anguish and Norwegian *anger*.

My biggest regret in life is that I was not listening out for those angels whispering to me that day. Pappa never came to the rescue, and what good is Pappa if he can't come to her rescue? What good is a *man* if he can't come to the rescue? What good is a man if he's just no good?

CHAPTER 5

It Shouldn't Take So Long to Hit a Duck

E ven though I was raised in the UK and my physical stays in the south of Italy were limited to six-week-long summer holidays, I cannot overemphasize how influential the Irpinian mountain hillbilly side of my culture was on my values and my moral compass. So, by the time I was in my midteens, I had learned that real men drove cars without a license and without seat belts. They made their own wine and appeared to enjoy drinking it, even if it tasted like old socks. They shot stray dogs without batting an eyelid. Real men built their own houses that they wouldn't sell for all the money in the world. And they made lots of children.

From a purely biological and evolutionary sense of the word, real men had one job to do: to procreate, inseminate, fertilize, pass on and fortify the gene pool, make offspring—preferably lots of them. My father made five of them. His father made seven. A man I sat next to once at dinner in Oman proudly informed me that he'd fathered nine children! He wore that number like a badge of honor on his chest.

Not until Olivia was born did I know for sure that I was able to fertilize a human egg in the way nature had intended it to be done. Not until Olivia joined the world was I sure that my man parts actually worked. Not until Olivia came into my life could I call myself *fully operative*.

Olivia was a branch of hope in an otherwise barren existence. She never knew that. She never knew what it took to bring her into this world. Our youngest daughter never knew just how much shit her mother and father had to go through so that she could even be born. I told myself that, one day, when she was old enough to understand, I would tell her why Olivia was the perfect name for her, how it meant peace and fertility. I promised myself that I would tell her what she meant to me—not only as a daughter but as living proof that I was a fully functioning male. Until the moment that Olivia was conceived, I had felt like a factory reject, a cheap bootleg replica of a man. Before Olivia came into my life, I could only call myself a man in a general sense. After she was born, though, *that's* when I could finally say I was a *real man*.

But I am getting a little ahead of myself. I need to go back to a doctor's office in Oslo thirteen years before that fateful summer's day in Puglia. The year was 2 BC—the letters BC standing for "before children" in this case. We didn't know at the time that it was the year *2 BC*, since we had only just started trying. All we knew was that getting pregnant was proving to be much more difficult than we could ever have imagined.

After almost two years of trying—not every second, admittedly, because that would be both exhausting and really antisocial—I had still not managed to impregnate my wife. We—and the doctors made a point of us using the term *we*—were still not pregnant. Only there was no *we* about it—at least, not in *my* head. Only the woman can actually get pregnant. Sure, we both play an important part in the act of creating new life, but our roles are quite different. *We* can't get pregnant; only *she* can. But it was my role to *get* her pregnant. It was abundantly clear to me that I was not fulfilling that role very well at all.

The initial tests revealed that my wife's reproductive system was pretty much intact. She had blood tests, Pap smear tests, urine tests, hormone tests, and a string of rather personal questions regarding her past and present sexual history. My stoic, no-nonsense Norwegian wife took it all in stride, never once complaining about having to go through so many more tests than me.

When it finally came to my turn, I tried to emulate my wife's stoicism and remain optimistic. But I had already arrived at the fairly obvious conclusion that it was me who was the weak link. This only served to accentuate my sense of frustration and inadequacy, my loneliness and incompetence. In true man style, though, I remained tight-lipped, stiffened my upper lip, and tried to seem unflappable. If I could feign enjoying my cousin's homemade Irpinian wine, then I could certainly pretend that my sense of masculinity was intact.

And then my fears were confirmed. The doctor delivered the news confirming that my man parts were not as fully operative as they should be. I was firing blanks. I was an incompetent, out-of-order man. At least, that's what it felt like to me at that moment. I was incompetent in the most primeval function that the male species has: the power to procreate. Not the *choice* to procreate but the *power*, the *ability*, the *capacity* to do so.

When you stop to consider that a man can produce anywhere between forty million and 1.2 *billion* sperm cells every time he ejaculates, it comes as quite a blow to hear that not a single one of your tiny sperm cells was able to hit their target. And remember, it only takes one. You would think they were pretty good odds, wouldn't you? Imagine standing at a shoot-the-duck fairground stall, and you get forty million chances to hit a duck. First prize is a human life. Let's say you manage to fire off one round every second, eight hours a day, nonstop, every single day. With forty million shots at your disposal, it would take you nearly two years to complete that task. If, by then, you hadn't managed to hit a duck, then you would have to be blind, be facing the wrong way, or have a serious physical disability, or all of the above. My point is, it shouldn't take so long to hit a duck.

The doctors told me that involuntary childlessness was quite common among couples, especially in this day and age, when couples started families much later in life than they used to. The modern, stressful lives that couples tended to lead these days were simply not conducive to getting pregnant. With as many as one in seven of the population wondering why they couldn't get pregnant, my wife and I were not alone, they reassured us.

I remember distinctly feeling that this statistic did little to make me feel any less alone. I could also sense that although my wife and I were in it together, we were also beginning to distance ourselves from each other emotionally. We were afraid of ending up childless. We were simply doing what people normally do when they are filled with fear and anxiety: We hid ourselves away in our own separate hiding places. We cowered from a looming truth we didn't want to accept.

What we should have done was have an honest, heartfelt, and vulnerable conversation with each other about how we felt. Knowing my wife like I know her today, she probably tried to make that happen on various occasions. But I wasn't receptive enough to her initiatives. I wasn't amenable to that type of conversation. That would have meant me opening myself up and making myself vulnerable, which was the opposite of what I'd been taught to do as a teenager. No, for me, there was only one way forward, one strategy: Grin and bear it. Show no fear.

Also around this time, the first tiny feelings of doubt started to creep into my mind about our compatibility for one another—my wife and me. Our loneliness was compounded by the fact that this was hardly something one went around sharing with other people. It's not really a topic for conversation around the dinner table, not even with friends. Can you imagine someone turning to you during dessert and saying, "Did you know I can't make children? You would think I would be able to hit a duck, wouldn't you, but I have blind, directionless sperm, with huge learning disabilities."

I felt frustrated and inadequate, inadequate and incompetent, small. No man wants to feel small—not in any department. At least I was not *totally* alone. I had my wife. We were in this together. That's what they kept telling us. That's what we told each other. It took two to tango, right? At least we could comfort each other, cry ourselves to sleep at night together.

We men can be pretty useless at a lot of things. You only need to observe the state of the planet to see that Mother Nature has been violated by predominantly male-dominated enterprises and nation states. Had women ruled the world, I doubt whether the damage would have been quite so calamitous. But for all our fallibilities, we men still have the one redeeming quality, one unique selling point, one thing that women actually can't do without us: the seed, the sperm, the 50 percent of the magic formula of life.

My God-given license to inseminate the opposite sex and increase the human race has been indefinitely revoked. I am inadequate. I am naked. I am raw. I am stoic. I hide my weakness. I am silent. I suppress my fear. I smother my anger.

But anger will always find a way to express itself. Like all toxic emotions, anger will always find a way out. It has to, because holding on to anger is as futile as trying to hold on to a burning coal. That coal will smolder away in the palm of your hand, sizzling your skin until you can't bear the pain anymore. You will have to release it, unleash it, like an Icelandic geyser spewing its sulfuric guts out into the atmosphere, spraying everything and everyone with its boiling geothermal plume.

As far as my own geothermal outbursts of anger are concerned, I know that they have affected the people I care about the most. I have driven them away. I have made it difficult for them to love me. Nobody in their right mind swallow dives into an Icelandic geyser, right? I know this. Cognitively, I get it.

For me, anger acts like a shield, an impenetrable shield that keeps people at a safe distance. Just like an Icelandic geyser keeps tourists at a safe distance without having to employ security guards or erect a fence. You just *know* not to step too close to that steaming sinkhole, for fear of your life. And as long as people are kept at a safe distance, they cannot do any harm to me. It sounds like a twisted kind of logic, I know, but it goes something like this.

Anger keeps people at a distance. And if people are kept at a distance, and if they are afraid to approach you or get too close to you, they can't get close enough to hurt you. In other words, anger is fear's protective armor. It's a kind of warped form of emotional risk management, albeit a lonely and painful one, because, of course, the long-term damage is that while people can't get close to you, they can't love you, either. I can deal with people seeing my anger; I just can't cope with people seeing my fear and my vulnerability.

Beards are also a great way to hide fear. Yes, you heard me correctly—beards! Take Genghis Khan, Hannibal, and Attila the Hun as examples. Apart from being expert warriors and slaughterers of men, women, and children, what did they all have in common? Beards. For sure, these beards helped to keep them warm during long winter nights, but they also made the heads of these warriors look that much bigger and fiercer, like the mane of a lion does. But there was another important function the beard had. Beards were an excellent way to disguise emotions from their adversaries in battle—emotions such as uncertainty, hesitation, self-doubt, and, of course, fear. The last thing you want on the battlefield is for your enemy to see fear on your face. A thick beard cleverly conceals a warrior's micro-expressions and emotions, especially emotions that could potentially make him look more vulnerable.

I have never been able to grow a beard. I've tried a few times. The last time I tried was during the COVID-19 lockdown of 2020. After two months of lockdown growth, just when I thought I was making some progress with my "beard," a friend of mine remarked, "Hey, I see you've started growing a beard. That will look really cool on you when you've given it a month or two."

I may not be able to grow a warrior-like beard, but I can certainly use anger. Anger is my way of masking fear.

CHAPTER 6

Let Them Hate, as Long as They Fear

St. Brendan's College was an all-boy Catholic grammar school in Bristol, England. It was run by a religious order known as the Christian Brothers. The religious order was of Irish descent, which explained why our teachers had names like O'Sullivan, MacMahon, Kelly, Callaghan, Kavanah, Malone, and Egan.

St. Brendan's prided itself on an education that was steeped in Catholic tradition. This was 1977, and I was in my second year of a seven-year stint at the school, so I'd had a full year to become properly acquainted with what "steeped in Catholic tradition" meant for the pupils: hard work and hard discipline.

Hard work inside the classroom ensured that everyone was made to believe that, with enough work and effort, you could go on to study at any university in Britain. Meanwhile, equally hard work *outside* the classroom produced star rugby and cricket players, many of whom went on to play for their county and country.

Hard discipline, meanwhile, came in the form of a generous helping of corporal punishment, seasoned with ample sprinklings of Catholic shame. The school's most common instrument for hard discipline was the leather strap, a twelve-inch long, two-inch wide, standard issue, hand-stitched brown leather belt shaped like the handle of a large basting brush. Only, instead of basting the breasts of succulent turkeys, these "Christian" brothers would baste the palms and buttocks of misbehaving, God-fearing Christian students.

The threshold for punishment was extremely low. A minor infraction like whispering to the person next to you during morning prayer would incur the wrath of any one of the dozen or so brothers who taught at the school. Discipline, discipline, discipline—that was what made men of boys. And they disciplined us *en masse* with their weapons of mass destruction, or should I say, weapons of *soul* destruction? Other weapons included twelve-inch rulers, training shoes, Bunsen burner tubes, bare knuckles on skulls, double-handed ear-thwacks, twisted ears, and, on the odd occasion, even fists.

We had a Latin teacher who demonstrated how effective the fist could be as an instrument not only of punishment but of learning and motivation, too. This Latin teacher's name was Mr. Ted McCarthy. The students called him Titch because he was so short; in fact, most of the pupils were taller than him.

One fine morning during Latin class, the boy next to me raised his hand and asked Titch McCarthy why we were wasting time studying Latin. The boy's name was Peter. After all, claimed Peter, nobody spoke Latin anymore. It was a dead language. A number of us nodded in approval.

Dead right, we thought. Dead wrong!

Titch McCarthy's response was swift, cruel, and remarkably erudite for a man dishing out such violence. Unbeknownst to Peter, Titch McCarthy was an amateur boxer, and before you could say "carpe diem," he'd grabbed my fellow thirteen-year-old pupil by his school tie, dragged him from his desk, rammed him up against the ropes—the row of cupboards that ran along the entire length of the classroom wall—and started pummeling him with left and right hooks.

That was the cruel and swift part. The erudite part was that, while he did this, he roared in Latin, "Cui bono?"

I actually understood this part. We'd recently learned this phrase in a passage we'd just studied by Cicero. It meant "What good is it for?"

"Cui bono?" Titch McCarthy roared again, his fists pumping back and forth like pistons, each one landing on its target with surgical precision.

Titch's next volley of erudite abuse I did *not* understand: "Oderint dum metuant!"

At the time, I figured he was saying something like, "Who the feckin' hell do you think you are? I'll show you what a dead language is, you little stuck-up snotbag!" although, in retrospect, it did seem like a few too many words to be conveyed in just three Latin words. Latin is certainly an efficient language, but not that efficient. It would be weeks before I plucked up the courage to ask Mr. McCarthy what he'd said to that poor boy, what *oderint dum metuant* meant.

"Let them hate, as long as they fear."

Apparently, these words were spoken by the infamous Roman emperor Caligula. He was a man of great ambition, which stood in stark contrast to his rather small physical stature. Caligula may have been small, but lack of height didn't stop him from fulfilling his big ambitions and often cruel conquests. Titch McCarthy was small too, but he had big punches. I often wondered whether Caligula would have been a more fitting nickname for Mr. McCarthy than Titch.

After Titch had finished basting Peter, he turned to the person sitting next to him—me—and glared.

"How about you, Riccardi?"

The teachers at our school always addressed us by our sur-names, never our first names. Either that or simply "Boy!"

"How about you, Riccardi? Do *you* think Latin is a dead language?"

Obviously not.

"Let me try to *e-lu-ci-date* you!" he roared, careful to enunciate each and every syllable of the word elucidate.

"Do you know what *elucidate* means, Riccardi?"

"N-n-no, sir. Sorry, sir. I don't."

"Aren't your parents Italian?" he roared.

"Y-y-yes, sir."

"What does the Italian word *luce* mean, then?" Titch's face was now so close to mine that I could see the pulsating veins in the corners of his eyes.

"Light, sir!"

"Good! And so does the *luci* part in *elucidate*. It means *light*. Elucidate means to cast light on, to explain."

Titch turned away from me to speak the rest of the class too, much to my relief. "Anyone know what *lucid* means?"

"Clear-headed, sir," came a surprisingly confident reply from the back of the classroom.

"Correct! *Compos mentis*—of sound mind. In other words, when you have light in your head, instead of the darkness most of you lot seem to have right now."

"Translucent!" boomed Titch again. Silence from the classroom.

"*Trans*, meaning 'through'; the light passes through it. Could Latin *be* more alive?" he boomed again.

Whether this form of teaching had any effect on poor Peter I will never know. However, on me, it had a profound effect. Suddenly, I started seeing Latin connections in so many words around me. Even Peter's name had a fantastic story behind it. It came from the Latin *pietra*, meaning rock. Jesus named his first pope Peter. (His real name was actually Simon, but Jesus renamed him when he said, "Thou art now Peter, and upon this rock I will build my church.") But the word has other connotations too. *Petrified* comes from the same Latin word: so scared that you have turned to stone.

It hadn't struck me there and then, but today, I understand that my petrified fellow student Peter could not have had a more appropriate name. The way he stood there pinned up against the ropes, as motionless and lifeless as a marble statue, battered and bruised, unable to move. It was as if Peter was holding his breath, playing dead, drowning quietly in an ocean of fear, hoping that his aggressor would lose interest in him and leave. How long could a fifteen-year-old hold his breath? How long could he block his *trachea*, to give it its Latinate name. Could he block it as long as Olivia could block hers?

· · ·

Our Catholic cruelty wasn't always directed from the top down. Several other students and I once played a practical joke on one of our classmates in chemistry class involving a Bunsen burner and a water tap. The victim was a boy who devoted his spare time to two pursuits: pumping iron and admiring himself in the mirror. There's nothing wrong with that, I guess. Most boys of that age are very conscious of their bodies.

Except that this particular boy had an insatiable need to show everyone how strong he was, how many chin-ups he could do in gym, how quickly he could climb a rope, how big his biceps were. And he insisted on wearing short-sleeved shirts, all year round, come rain or shine. His shirts were always a little too tight so he could really accentuate his bulges. I don't remember his real name, just his nickname. We called him Om, as in the French *homme*, meaning "man." We left out all the unnecessary silent letters and substituted them with a generous serving of irony and disdain.

Om was another young man raised to believe that the way to attract friends and admirers was to be the alpha male: tough and unbeatable. Om was desperately trying to fit in with the crowd, to become one of the pack. He was looking for a sense of belonging, desperately trying to be accepted. I guess he figured that the more he emulated other male role models of the time, the more he would be accepted by his peers. After all, the male role models around us in those days at the end of the 1970s were mostly to be found on TV: James Bond, Dirty Harry, the Six Million Dollar Man, Superman. All of them were tough, invincible alphas. Om was just doing what any young, insecure, desperate teenage boy would do. Well, it didn't work. He just ended up being a loner. Plus, he was really short—an easy target, in other words.

One of my classmates took a Bunsen burner and heated up the water tap to the point right before when it would start to glow red. It was one of those classic British cross-handle taps with the four rounded ends. Then we called Om over, under the pretense that we weren't strong enough to loosen the tap. Could he help us weaklings, please?

It was like offering candy to a six-year-old. Over he came, strutting, his biceps, triceps, and forearms already flexed and bulging out of his short-sleeved shirt, ready for action. He may even have thought that he was finally about to win friends and admirers.

What came next was not a pretty sight. For weeks afterward, Om's palm had a four-star tattoo, one that had been seared into his skin. Over time, that tattoo peeled, healed, peeled, and re-healed in seemingly endless cycles.

It's certainly not something I am proud of today, even if it wasn't me who was directly responsible for the incident. I didn't stop the bullying, either. I could explain it away as bowing down to peer pressure, and you might even buy my excuse, but the fact is that, as I retell this story, I am overcome with a deep sense of regret and shame for what I did to Om. I wish I could remember his real name so I could track him down and ask for his forgiveness.

. . .

A few weeks later, I was caught by my chemistry teacher passing a note to a friend during the exam. I was given instant detention and ordered to see the teacher after school. Our chemistry teacher's name was Derek. At least that's what all the students called him. That may or may not have been his real name. As you can imagine, a teacher's nickname was often very different from his or her real name, such as Handlebars, Fiddler, Froggy, Ticker, Wetleg, and Ripper. T.C. was a good one. They were his actual initials, plus he was the headmaster, which made him the Top Cat, hence T.C. Another clever nickname was Brock, which was short for Broccoli. Why Broccoli? Well, his real name was Brother Kelly, which, in its written form became Bro. Kelly. BroKelly. Get it? That nickname always made me smile, even if the person whose nickname it was did not make me smile at all.

Derek was a disciplinarian, a staunch supporter of tough education, the very personification of a teacher "steeped in Catholic tradition." Teachers like Derek were the reason the British government introduced the ban on corporal punishment in schools in 1986. But this wasn't 1986 yet; this was 1977, and Derek was renowned for his enthusiasm and obvious delight every time he had the opportunity to punish a pupil.

We were all terrified of Derek, with his corduroy jacket and his woolly tank top, and his thick, black prescription spectacles that he would have to remove before administering a beating. Such was the vigor and the vitriol in his swing. Derek seemed devoid of feelings and compassion for the human spirit. His eyes were as cold and glassy as the laboratory test tubes that we used in our experiments. Chemistry seemed to be the perfect subject for Derek to teach: formulas and periodic tables, predictable, predetermined, with the propensity to be explosive and caustic when provoked. But worse than that, Derek was a sadistic cunt.

He would parade himself around the classroom with the swagger of a person who was fully aware of what privileges his rank, uniform, and institutional connections afforded him. Because without them, the schoolboys he systematically terrorized would have ripped him to shreds, and Derek would have suffered the same fate as the likes of Mussolini, Gaddafi, and Saddam Hussein.

So, when I was told to see him after school, I knew what was coming. I knew I would be subjected to his special brand of cuntish reprimand.

Derek's preferred weapon of mass soul destruction was the standard-issue leather strap. No surprise there. Like Derek, it was predictable, predetermined, explosive, and caustic. Normally, Derek would administer the punishment by holding the pupil's wrist with his left hand while strapping the pupil's hand with his right. However, for the particularly heinous crime of cheating in an exam, I would be receiving special treatment, a little twist, a bespoke form of pain. Perhaps that's why he asked me to see him after school, because then he knew nobody would be around to witness the fact that not only was he a sadistic cunt, but he was a sadistic cunt with a vivid imagination.

Aside to the reader: I am sensing that you may have balked at my use of the c-word to describe a former teacher of mine. Perhaps you're thinking, however much the author disliked the man, surely he could have picked another, less abrasive, or even less offensive term of derision for him, like bastard or dickhead or prick. Allow me to explain the rationale behind my choice. First of all, cunt is the only word that comes even close to capturing the hatred I had for this person. And second, from a purely linguistic point of view, when I say the word cunt out loud, with its voiceless velar plosive at the beginning and its voiceless alveolar stop at the end, it is the only combination of consonants and short vowels that accurately encapsulates the contempt I had for that man.

Derek instructed me to place my hand on top of the lab worktop, right next to where the Bunsen burner gas taps were, with my palm facing up. He was specific about that. Palm up. I remember thinking how rough the work surface felt on the back of my hand from all the chemical spillages and acid burns the students had caused during experiments. I remember thinking that if there was a work surface under my hand, then there would be nothing below my hand to cushion the blow, no give or flex in my wrist to dissipate some of the force. It would be like a car driving into an oak tree: sixty to naught in point one of a second, the total transfer of energy from an inanimate moving object to an inanimate stationary object. We'd studied this phenomenon in our physics class. I couldn't remember the formula or the exact figures, but I did remember being astounded at the enormous g-force this resulted in.

I wondered if the searing heat that was about to be generated in the palm of my own hand would compare to the heat Om felt from the tap. Either way, as Derek steadied his body and his aim, his arm raised high into the air, his leather strap quivering like the tongue of a snake as it prepares to strike, I braced myself for a level of heat and pain I knew would leave an indelible mark on my hand and my soul. Perhaps this was just karma for my awful complicit act of cruelty to Om—in which case, fair dos.

Three times Derek struck on each hand, with all his weight, with all his vitriolic disdain for the human spirit. By the end of his thrashing, he was actually out of breath, his small, insignificant, tank-top-covered chest heaving in time with the throbbing of my palms. As he placed his cheap spectacles back on his nose, I inspected my hands: a two-inch wide purple streak across each palm, plus an extra stripe across one of my wrists, where he'd slightly missed the target in his overzealous attempt to sink all his body weight into the blow.

Derek glared at me for a few seconds as his eyes readjusted to the 20/20 vision of his spectacles. He seemed somewhat forlorn, disappointed even. I'd like to think that it was because I had not shed a single tear for him. I knew it would hurt—and it really did fucking hurt—but I was determined not to cry.

Imagine if it got out to all my friends that I'd cried. Derek could easily have leaked that kind of information, and that would have immediately sent me tumbling down the classroom pecking order. I was not going to let that happen. I wasn't about to cry now, not for Derek. I wanted to. I *really* wanted to, but it was the only way I could say "fuck you" to Derek. Oderint dum metuant? No fucking way, Derek! I may hate you, but I do not fear you.

What I *did* fear, though, even as my palms pulsated with the afterglow of Derek's thrashing, was the hungry, sleep-deprived night-shift father who was waiting for me to come home so that he could eat. That, and the final words Derek said to me before he dismissed me from his classroom.

"And don't let me catch you cheating again, boy! You hear me?"

"Yes, sir. No, sir. Can I go now, sir?"

"Uh, yes. . . . You can go. Yes, go, Riccardi."

He'd tried to humiliate me, to subject me to a level of violence that after 1986 would have him sent to jail, and he'd failed. Sure, he'd left a couple of stripes on my hand, but they would be gone in a day or two, unlike poor Om's star-shaped tattoos.

Chapter 7

Butt Stuff

There's something inherently suspect about allowing someone to explore a part of your body you haven't even had the opportunity to be acquainted with yourself. My asshole is the one part of my body I have never actually seen with my own eyes. Nor has anyone else. Well, my mother and father have seen it, yes, but that was when I was a baby. Nobody has ever seen my asshole in its current fully-grown adult state. In fact, there can't be many other men who can claim to have seen their own asshole. The anus lies outside your natural field of view, unless you happen to have the neck of a giraffe. If you were to have a police lineup of various assholes, where one of them was my own, I wouldn't have a clue. I wouldn't be able to tell one brown starfish from the other. A man's own asshole is as mysterious as a black hole in outer space and will remain that way as long as we have no reason to explore down there.

The next stage of confirming my inability to procreate involved finding out just how blind, directionless, and disabled my swimmers really were. This is how I ended up on an examination table at the Andrology Centre in Oslo, wearing a flimsy gown. The gown was open in the back, and so was I.

I had to actually look up the word *andrology*; it means "specific to men." I never knew that the list of diseases and conditions specific to men could be so long: everything from erectile dysfunction to premature ejaculation, from prostate examinations to cystoscopies and urinary tract infections, circumcisions, testosterone deficiency, low libidos, and, finally, the reason why I was there, infertility problems.

That there was actually an entire clinic dedicated to male issues in such a relatively small city like Oslo confirmed to me that I was not alone. And yet, despite the statistical evidence, my sense of isolation and loneliness persisted, overpowering and weighing on my rational mind like a bad hangover. No matter how much I tried to rationalize my predicament, the voice in my head was stuck on repeat, telling me the same thing over and over again: You are not a real man.

So there I was, lying on the examination table, on my side, in a semifetal position, facing the wall, contemplating not only how forlorn I must have looked but also how ridiculous. I was about to be subjected to a rectal prostate examination. I was naked from the waist down, except for my socks. I don't really know why I kept my socks on. Perhaps in the hope that it would help me retain a modicum of dignity. But let's be honest: There really is no dignity in a rectal examination, is there?

I am pretty sure that the stench of my fear seeped through

the cracks of my angry armor and into the room, where the doctor softly whistled a tune to himself. It was a chirpy, breathy, staccato whistle that sounded like a set of cheap Peruvian pan-pipes: jolly, nonchalant, yet oddly reassuring. He sounded like a window cleaner, whistling while he worked.

I feel vulnerable—really vulnerable. And I am afraid, actually. I am afraid of what the doctor will find when he explores my plumbing. That's what the doctor keeps calling my reproductive system—plumbing. Why can't he just call it what it is? My reproductive system. My prostate. My testicles. My sperm sack. His euphemism reminds me of that quintessential British staple of social interaction, understatement. You know, when a Brit says to you, "I guess that's another way of looking at it," when he really means "Your idea sucks!" I've always seen British understatement as not only a vague form of communication—mysterious and unfathomable to most nonnative speakers of English, in fact—but also a cowardly one too. British understatement undermines the number-one rule of communication: clarity.

The doctor's euphemism, as well intentioned as it may be, only serves to add another emotion to my fear and sense of vulnerability—anger. Yes, I'm angry now, too. Alone, ridiculous, inadequate, incompetent, angry. Fuck, I'm angry! Angry at his euphemisms, angry at how I ended up on this examination table, angry at the fact that everything seemed so much easier before I got married and decided to start a family, and angry at being an immigrant in Norway, the country that my wife *explicitly* promised would make me happy.

Anger is not good for you. It is a toxic emotion. Left unchecked, anger will gnaw away at the very core of your soul, corroding it, inflaming it, scarring it like cheap vodka on an alcoholic's liver. Anger burns too, from the inside out. I could feel its embers glowing inside me as the doctor explained to me what he was going to do. I don't quite know why I was so angry or where all this inner anger was coming from. But it was there, constantly simmering below the surface. What I didn't know at the time was that this anger would one day rear its ugly head and make me do something that I would regret forever, to the person I least wanted to do it to.

I can't believe I am paying this doctor Harley Street rates to do what he is about to do to me. It's a good job I am lying facing the wall with my back to him, so at least I don't have to expend precious energy pretending I am okay. That's what we men are often very good at: pretending we are okay, that we're in control, when really, we are not.

There are two posters on the wall, just inside my field of view: one depicting all the different muscle groups of a human body and the other a cross-section diagram of a man's plumbing. I focus on the poster with the plumbing. It helps distract me from the clinking and clanking of the various medical instruments the doctor is tinkering with behind me.

"Everything okay there, Mr. Riccardi?" the doctor asks me.

"Everything okay," I reply.

But I am not okay. I am scared, and vulnerable, and angry. Not just with the examination I am about to have but the whole reason why I am here in the first place. Four words keep echoing in my head:

I

Cannot

Make

Babies

The reverb of the last syllable of *babies* dissipates into the recesses of my mournful mind, sending me into a quasi-dreamlike state, when suddenly I hear from behind me the unmistakably sharp snap of a pair of latex gloves and I am wrenched back to reality—that reality being that a doctor is about to get to the bottom of things (pun intended). That's when I recognize the tune the doctor is whistling: an irritatingly catchy hit record of the time by Eve and Gwen Stefani called "Let Me Blow Ya Mind." How fitting. I am definitely about to have my mind blown all right.

"Try to relax, Mr. Riccardi. You'll enjoy it a lot more if you relax," the doctor continues with his indefatigable window cleaner chirpiness. "Now then, what I am about to do is insert this TRUS into you."

"A what?"

"A TRUS. Sorry, that's short for transrectal ultrasound. What it does is it gives me an image of your prostate gland and any-thing else that might be going on in your plumbing. Completely standard procedure."

"Okay, Doctor. Well, I guess my TRUS is in your hands then, eh?"

"Very good, Mr. Riccardi. Very good."

I managed to get a smile out of this doctor. Perhaps he'll go a little easier on me. I hope so.

. . .

The last and only time I remember anyone putting something up my bum was when I was ten years old. I was spending the summer with my grandparents in Italy at the time, and this particular day we had spent at the beach.

This was 1974, the same year that the sun protection factor system was introduced on a wide scale—factor 10, factor 20, and so on—and general awareness of the harmful effects of overexposure to the sun was increasing. Not that that mattered to my father.

"When you get-a hot, you can-a lie down under da umbarella, innit! The sun cream is just another way for a-the men with a-the power to make-a more money, innit! And anyway, I never used it as a kid, innit!"

My parents often finished their sentences with the word *innit*. *Innit* was the immigrant's conveniently universal tag question that substituted for a myriad of other tag questions one found in the English language, like *doesn't it? don't they? aren't they?* and so forth. This was something many immigrants in the UK did, especially the European ones. Today, the word *innit* has become an integral part of what is commonly referred to as MLE, or Multicultural London English.

We didn't get any sun cream, and by midmorning the wind had picked up so much that we had to take down our parasol. The wind also provided us with a false sense of security by cooling down our bodies as we splashed around in the sea, so by the time we came home, we were all pretty barbecued. I was particularly sizzled and soon began feeling nauseous and feverish, telltale signs of heat stroke and exposure.

My mother decided that the most urgent course of action was to get my fever under control. She could do that in one of two ways.

Option number 1 was an acetaminophen injection. This is effective but should only be administered by a doctor or trained nurse. It was nighttime by now, and the doctor's surgery was closed.

"Can't you call the doctor? He lives in the same building as his surgery, Mamma."

"No, I don't want to disturb *il dottore* now. And anyway, it costs double when you visit him after normal hours, innit."

"What's option number 2?"

"A suppository."

"A what?"

"A suppository. It-a works just as a-well, and it's-a chip, innit."

"It's a chip? A potato?" I cried out without any irony in my voice whatsoever.

"Not chip. Chiiip!" she replied. "You know, it no cost as-a much."

Suppository it was then.

I'd never seen a suppository before. Up until that moment, all I'd ever been administered by way of pain relief or fever reduction had been either in liquid form or dissolvable tablets, and both of these came in fruity flavors like strawberry or banana.

I lay down on my bed, shaking with fever and trepidation as my mother removed the suppository from its aluminum packaging. It looked like a white bullet to a very large handgun, the kind Clint Eastwood would tote around in his *Dirty Harry* movies. Then my mother started smearing that torpedo-shaped suppository with olive oil. Lubrication. Then she took aim.

Like many kids of the 1960s and '70s who were raised in an environment still reminiscent of Victorian England, we had a repressed attitude to certain body parts and body noises. Burping, farting, peeing, and pooing were simply not mentioned out loud. One simply didn't do that, did one? We still used expressions like *willy* for penis and *tuppence* or even *front bottom* for vagina, which I thought was really odd, considering what normally comes out of any bottom. Plus, we were Catholic. We believed in concepts like original sin and the Immaculate Conception. Put Victorianism and Catholicism into the same socially repressive cocktail mix, and you have the perfect recipe for unprecedented anal retentiveness.

All I remember is my mother squishing her index finger into my bum hole trying to insert that goddamn bullet-shaped suppository past the sphincter muscle so that it could begin to absorb into my intestine and deal with my fever.

All I had to do was allow my sphincter to open up. Instead, I boarded up that asshole like a Mississippi shopkeeper boards up his windows before an impending hurricane. The more she struggled to insert the tablet, the tighter I clenched. The suppository would go inside but not far enough to allow the sphincter muscle to contract again. Instead, my sphincter would literally spit the suppository back out again in protest, like a child who refuses to eat his greens. "I don't *like* broccoli! You eat it!"

She started yelling at me. I yelled back at her. It was messy, metaphorically and literally. She never did get that suppository past that sphincter muscle, though, and from that moment on, that part of my body would be by invitation only, a holy sanctuary, a maximum-security safe haven for only my most intimate of acquaintances, special people with the highest security clearance. From that moment on, my asshole would be my body's Oval Office—or, should I say, Oval *Orifice*.

. . .

Back at the Andrology Centre, the doctor is hovering around my Oval Orifice, but I am still a little unsure as to whether he should be given top-level security clearance. As I lie there facing the wall, I am drawn to the posters again—in particular, the one of the cross-section diagram of a man's pelvic area, where each vital part of this plumbing system is tagged with a Latin name. I can't find the word sphincter, though. Strange.

Perhaps if I read the Latin names to myself, it will take my mind off that really annoying panpipe whistling behind me. I start with *symphysis pubis*. Moving on to *corpus cavernosum*. Then *corpus spongiosum*. Penile urethra. Scrotum. Testis, prostate, anus. *Rectum! What the fuck was that? Security breach! Security breach!* My sphincter is under attack. I repeat: My sphincter . . . is under . . . attack!

Something has just entered my anal passage. It feels bigger and harder than a finger but smaller and less rigid than a baseball bat. And it's making a soft squelchy sound. Why is it squelching? How far up is he actually *going*? According to the diagram on the wall, it should be about four centimeters. This feels more like four meters!

"Try to relax, Mr. Riccardi."

"It's a bit hard to relax when someone is driving the wrong way up a one-way street, Doctor."

No reaction from the doctor. He seems concentrated, focused. He's stopped whistling. He's wiggling about inside me. It lasts for about a minute, but it's a minute too long, as far as I am concerned.

"Okay, Mr. Riccardi, if you can just breathe in deeply for me . . . and breathe out."

Before I could fully exhale, whatever was *in* my rectum has suddenly been ejected *from* my rectum. Accompanying the ejection was the same squelching sound I'd heard upon entry, followed by a sound that I can only best describe as a sloppy fanny fart.

And now something is trickling down my left buttock—warm, gooey, slimy. Oh, God! What *is* that? Surely not, I whimper to myself. Have I . . . ? Have I . . . ? Have I *shit* myself?

The doctor is whistling again, though. He wouldn't be doing that if I had shat myself. He's not that chirpy. Besides, it doesn't smell like shit. It smells like . . . What *is* that smell? It smells like . . . windscreen wiper fluid! Alcohol?

Still whistling, the good doctor hands me a large clump of paper towel. It's the kind you would pull from an industrial paper towel dispenser at a mechanic's workshop—handy if you need to soak up gooey puddles of oil from the workshop floor. *Wow! That's a lot of paper*, I think. *How much is there to clean up?*

Without saying a word, I take the paper towel and press it gently onto my breached rear end. Then, carefully, and surprisingly gracefully for a man who has just been violated, I swivel my whole body around, drop my legs over the side of the examination table, and stand up, making sure that I do not let go of the paper towel pressed firmly against my dripping asshole.

As I wipe, I glance down at the paper. To my relief, the paper is not stained with anything brown but with a blue medical lubricant gel the doctor used to smear the optical rectal probe, which he is now wiping clean with the same industrial paper towel. I'm quite surprised at the relative slenderness and elegance of the probe and relieved that it does not have the girth of a baseball bat.

CHAPTER 8

Sugar Daddy

My father began working at the chocolate factory in September 1971, ten years after he'd emigrated to the UK. Since that foggy March day in 1961, when he first set foot on British soil, my father had spent years job-hopping. From the textile mills of Lancashire and Derbyshire, he headed south to try his hand at various heavy industry factories in Somerset and Wiltshire. He even had a stint at the now defunct Marcos car factory in Bradford-on-Avon. Finally, he settled for a job at the world-famous chocolate manufacturer, Cadbury's, at their factory in a small town just outside Bristol. That small town was called Keynsham.

Keynsham would have probably remained completely unknown to the outside world had it not been for Cadbury's. A roadside sign as you enter the town reminds you of the importance of the chocolate manufacturer: "Welcome to Keynsham—sponsored by Cadbury's."

Imagine sponsoring a whole town! That very same sign had a second part to it: "Eat More Chocolate," as if Keynsham's very existence depended on the world's ability to stuff its face with cocoa extract and sugar.

Within the confines of these red-bricked walls, my father has had to endure the brain-numbing tedium of packing chocolates into boxes, something he does in a three-phase rotational shift schedule of early mornings, afternoons, and nights, day after day, night after night, ever since he packed his first bar of chocolate.

Hygiene standards in the factory require him to wear a specific type of uniform. It's a standard-issue Cadbury's uniform of a white hip-length jacket, white trousers, white clogs, and a white hair net that looks like a flimsy shower cap. It's a very different type of attire to, say, a fireman, or a mechanic, or an offshore oil worker, all jobs where men look tough and dirty.

My father never showed me his work clothes, at least not while he was wearing them. I only saw them hanging on the washing line at home after they'd been washed. I did see how other Cadbury employees were dressed, though, when my father brought home a company magazine once. It didn't take too much imagination to picture my father in the same clothes. And it required even less imagination to know that my father would have hated those clinically white garments.

He would have hated those clothes as much as he hated his job, his numbingly lonely, unfulfilling job.

The only reason he worked this rotation of shift work was because it paid slightly more than normal daytime working hours. The factory has to keep producing chocolate around the clock in order to supply the world's insatiable craving for comfort food, hence the extra incentive pay for those who are willing to work all three production time slots.

However, no amount of money will fool the biological rhythms of the body into believing that irregular sleeping patterns are good for it, especially sleeping during the day.

Every month, my father would pick up his salary in a brown envelope and place those measly extra pounds, shillings, and pence he'd been paid for his nocturnal grind into a special savings account. The primary purpose of that savings account was not so much a "for a rainy day" account as it was "for a month of sunshine back home with my family in Italy" account. As my father astutely commented, if he'd dipped into that account every time it rained in England, he'd be bankrupt by now.

It took him two years to save up enough money to be able to treat himself to a trip back to his homeland. He would have traveled back to Italy every year if he could afford it, but he couldn't. Not on his shitty salary, if you could even call it a salary.

Every third week, my father and I would catch a glimpse of each other in the early hours of the morning in the kitchen. He would be drinking a cup of tea before heading for his pillow, while I would be hurrying down my Rice Krispies or Frosties before heading off for the school bus.

Occasionally, we would exchange a mumbled *buongiorno*, but mostly we avoided each other's glances and conversations. It was best that way. I knew that my father had a short fuse at the best of times, and that fuse was certainly no longer after working the night shift in clogs and a hair net.

I never quite understood why he was like that, especially when he saw me heading for school. I mean, that's why he'd emigrated in the first place, right? To provide better opportunities for himself and his family.

If there was anything about his childhood that had severely disadvantaged his adult life, it was his lack of education. Or, at least, the lack of *opportunity* to get educated. By moving to a country like England, he was ensuring that his children didn't end up in the same scarcity and poverty trap.

Surely, seeing his son go off to a great school would have inspired him to carry on in his crappy job—a "this is why I do it" mentality. Alas, those few times our gazes met, his face carried more of "is *this* why I do it?" expression. That never made sense to me.

Anyway, soon after our muted encounter, my father would collapse into bed while I would slump into the seat of a no. 339 bus and settle in for the hour-long ride to school. That bus route took me past the same Cadbury factory in Keynsham. Every school day, I would be reminded of my father's brain-dead job.

The factory was a nondescript, red brick building from 1935 that was perched over the banks of the River Chew, its giant *Cadbury's* sign suspended five stories above the main entrance. Inside the factory, hundreds of white-clad men and women would produce some of the biggest global brands of chocolate in the world. Crunchie, Flake, Curly Wurly, Dairy Milk, Double Decker, Turkish Delight, and the iconic Cadbury Creme Egg.

I would often peer through the fogged-up windows of the bus and think that this factory my father worked in looked nothing like the chocolate factory Charlie Bucket walked past every day. Sure, it had the iron gates and the smoke-belching chimneys that Roald Dahl wrote about, and there were probably even strange whizzing sounds that came from deep inside it. From where I was sitting, though, on the top deck of that badly ventilated double-decker bus from the 1970s, there was little hint that the air "for half a mile around in every direction . . . was scented with the heavy rich smell of melting chocolate," to quote Roald Dahl.[1] All I could smell on that bus to school was the pungent cocktail of testosterone and teenage angst that oozed from the armpits of a hundred Catholic teenage boys.

Summers in England were a painful reminder of how far away my father was from his own parents and also how little financial benefit his move to another country had actually afforded him. For years, he'd made excuses to his family about why he didn't travel down to see them every year, how difficult it was to get so much time off. It wasn't true; the factory closed every summer for maintenance. He'd explain how he had nobody to water his vegetables for him while he was gone. Really? Isn't England a self-watering country? He argued that the clutch on his car had played up and they couldn't get hold of the spare parts. Again, this was unlikely when you drive a Ford, one of the most commonly owned family cars in the world.

Flying to Italy was out of the question. Flying was far too expensive. And anyway, where would he put all the presents that he'd brought over for family and friends?

---

1 Roald Dahl, *Charlie and the Chocolate Factory* (New York: Puffin Books, 2013), 7.

My father always made sure to bring clothes back to Italy with him in the car, which he would then distribute to friends and family. Back in his village, children would roam the streets barefoot, so clothes were a welcome gift. My father would load the car with these "gifts" for his family. They were not new clothes, but clothes that his children had grown out of, hand-me-downs from England to provide a helping hand for friends and family still struggling to make ends meet back home.

My father's charity was also an excellent way to communicate his sense of prosperity in the New Country. The more clothes he gave away, the more generous—and therefore prosperous—his family thought he was.

He'd pile sack loads of clothes in the car—so many, in fact, that we would have to stuff the foot wells of the car behind the driver and passenger seats with them, forcing my sister and me in the back of the car to sit with our knees tucked up under our chins. It was a horribly uncomfortable position to sit, not to speak of how lethal it would have been if we'd crashed. Then again, we didn't have seat belts anyway. Our only consolation was that, whenever we wanted to take a nap, one of us could lie full length along the foot wells on a "mattress" of clothes bags. It was quite comfortable, actually. We took a lot of naps.

In addition to the clothes, he would always take one extra suitcase, an extra special suitcase filled with an important "luxury" item, a nonessential, nonutilitarian commodity that communicated to his family back home in Italy how prosperous a life he led in his new country. That luxury item was chocolate. If he could not bring with him the actual milk and honey of his new life, then at least he could bring something just as sweet and delicious: chocolate—lots of chocolate.

What was special about these particular chocolates was that they had no wrapping paper on them. This was because these chocolates were factory rejects, chocolates that, for whatever reason, could not be sold to the public, either because they had been cut too short or too long or because they were slightly out of shape or because the chocolate hadn't been mixed quite right or because they had been dropped onto the factory floor by accident. These rejects would then be gathered into huge bins, before being wrapped up in bundles of ten, like kindling, to be sold off in the factory tuck shop at a fraction of the cost of the real product. My father would buy these deformed bundles of Crunchie bars and Curly Wurlys, bring them home, and put them straight into storage in a cool, dark place.

Now and then, he would let us have a bar or two as a treat. "It-a taste just-a like-a da real thing, innit?" he would say to us. He was right. It did taste just as good as the ones with wrapping paper on them.

Just before the departure date for our summer holiday, my father would take all the chocolate he had hoarded up and pack them all into an old PVC suitcase, which he would then hoist up onto the roof rack of the car, the only place where it would fit, since the rest of the car was stuffed with clothes and his children. He'd done this a couple of times, so by the time he prepared his suitcase of chocolate for the 1976 trip, friends and family were waiting in anticipation for the arrival of the Sugar Daddy from England.

But 1976 was not like any other year. There was a severe heat wave that year in the UK. That summer saw the second hottest average temperatures since records began. In the southwest of England where I grew up, some areas went for forty-five days without rain! The UK government passed the Drought Act in the same year, which gave them enormous powers to restrict how much water people used at home. It was so hot that summer that the death rate in the UK rose by over 20 percent. And if it was that hot in the UK, you can imagine how hot it would be in Italy.

So, for three days and three nights, which is the time it took us to drive the 2,300 kilometers to my grandparents' home in the south, that suitcase was subjected to temperatures of forty-plus Celsius by day and left to cool at night. It was a PVC casserole dish by day, turning those paperless chocolate bars into a boiling, simmering fondue of brown mush. By night, those chocolates congealed into a solid breeze-block of brown cement. Crunchies and Curly Wurlys had been melded into Crunchie Wurlys. Flakes and Double Deckers had fused into Flaky Deckers.

For the first week of our summer holidays, my mother spent her days painstakingly separating the Crunchie from the Wurly, and the Flaky from the Decker, so that when my father gave the chocolate to his family, they would look half presentable.

You may be asking yourself, why did it have to be my mother who performed this task and not my father? The chocolates were mostly for *his* family, after all, not hers. Was it because my mother had smaller fingers to better pry open and separate the chocolates from one another? Not at all. The real reason was more subtle than that. She did it because she wanted to. Volunteering to separate the chocolates was one of many ways she showed appreciation for my father for putting up with such a shitty job, working nights, and earning a little extra just so he could provide for his family and save up enough money so that all of them could travel back to Italy. My mother worked too. She contributed to the family's bank account too. She was not a stay-at-home mother. Her job was in the kitchen of a private boarding school, preparing food and washing up. If her paycheck had been as posh as the school, my father would never have needed to work those extra night shifts. Besides, she not only got to see his family; she got to see *hers* too.

Volunteering to separate the chocolates had another equally important function. It helped alleviate my father's deep sense of inadequacy as provider and protector for the family. In his eyes, a proper provider would not only take his family back to Italy every year, but he would do it with a suitcase of chocolates that still had their wrappers on them. At least then, even if they got stewed on their way there, they would look like individual brown ingots of world-famous chocolate rather than a slab of unrecognizable gunk.

When I recall this episode, I don't think that my mother was submissive or subservient or "sub" anything. I just think how noble of her this was, how loving, how empathic. My mother knew that my father had done a foolish thing. I mean, who on earth puts a suitcase of chocolate on a car roof and drives it for three days in the boiling hot sun to one of the hottest regions of the Mediterranean and *not* expect it to arrive there as one big slab of mush? She hadn't argued with him before they'd set off on their long journey. She never even said, "Well, what did you think was going to happen?" or "I told you so!" after the fact. No. My father had been a fool. He'd made a silly mistake. It was not an end-of-the-world mistake, but it was a big enough mistake for him to feel really foolish, to feel that he had lost his *bella figura*. My mother knew that. And my father knew that she knew that *he* knew that.

But that deep sense of inadequacy never completely left my father. It was always there, like a pilot light on a gas fire. However much my mother tried to extinguish that flame, that pilot light of rage kept on flickering in his very soul. All it took was the tiniest of sparks to turn that pilot light into an inferno.

CHAPTER 9

Masturbato, Ergo Sum

B ack at the Andrology Centre, I am idly flicking through a copy of *National Geographic*, waiting my turn. I am there to provide a sperm sample. *There's a first time for everything, I guess,* I say to myself, hoping immediately that I haven't just said that out loud. I am trying to be positive and pragmatic about the whole thing. Keep your eye on the prize, and all that. The uncomfortable episode with the TRUS is behind me and no longer *in* my behind.

The clinic is full of men, predominantly middle-aged, all of whom are deliberately avoiding eye contact with each other. If this had been post-2010, these men would all have had the perfect socially accepted alibi to *not* look at each other—a mobile device. Then they could have swiped away to their hearts' content, checking their news feeds and social media notifications. Instead, this pre-2010 gathering of ungainly aspirants has to make do by either gazing aimlessly into a distant corner of the room or into one of the many dog-eared magazines strewn across the large coffee table—magazines about cars, boats, hunting, fishing, and one copy of *National Geographic.* We're definitely not at a hair salon, that's for sure.

The man opposite me looks up and catches my eye for a microsecond. His glance is too fleeting and momentary to be interpreted as an invitation to engage with him, but it was definitely long enough for us both to feel a little awkward. Instinctively, we both avert our attention elsewhere, which, in my case, is back to the magazine on my lap.

My grateful gaze falls on a full-page photo of a man dressed in a white coat and a hygiene cap similar to the one my father used to wear in the chocolate factory. The man is perched over a large leg of ham, one hand placed lovingly on the thickest part of the thigh, his other hand inserting a long, needle-like instrument deep into the muscle of the leg. Judging by the man's jet-black hair and bushy moustache, I conclude he must be southern European or Middle Eastern. On second thought, no, he can't be from the Middle East, not if he's massaging a slab of pork. The caption below the photo confirms my Sherlock Holmes instincts:

> An inspector from the Istituto Parma Qualità (IPQ) inserts a porous horse bone needle into the leg of the ham at five critical points, then smells the needle with his finely tuned nose to check for that distinctive Parma ham "sweetness."

I look up again. Still no eye contact with anyone. I almost want to let out a little "Huh! You don't say!"—the kind that implicitly invites anyone else within earshot to inquire what it is that I am reading that is so fascinating, as if I am a character in the film *Pleasantville* or something. But the atmosphere is all wrong for that kind of exchange, so, instead, I make a mental note to myself to draw a cartoon thought bubble above my head. Best to keep my thoughts to myself.

Sweetness? I thought Parma ham was salty. And why does it have to be a horse bone needle? Does it matter if it is a donkey bone needle?

I am intrigued and delve deeper into the article. There I discover that in order to preserve Parma ham's reputation as a *sweet* ham, you need to employ the skills of a *maestro salatore*, or salt master, whose job it is to cure the meat with salt. The *maestro salatore's* unique skill lies in knowing *exactly* how and when to apply *exactly* the right amount of sea salt, under *exactly* the right atmospheric conditions, for *exactly* the right amount of time. Nothing is left to chance. None of the taste of a true *Parma* ham is accomplished by accident. If the *maestro salatore* has done his job well, he will earn the ham producer the highly coveted official IPQ stamp, the five-point ducal crown, or Parma Crown.

And the horse bone needle?

I never actually find an answer to my question. All the same, it's the kind of trivia I love, and normally, I would share it with anyone willing to listen, like the person sitting opposite me in a waiting room.

I glance up again briefly. All eyes in the room are pointed in every which way imaginable, except toward any other eyes. Their roaming reminds me of dozens of lighthouses scanning the night sky, warning others to keep their distance.

The Parma ham article sets off a series of associations in my brain. I have family in Parma, migrants like my mother and father who ended up in the factories of industrialized northern Italy rather than northern England.

Parma was also where neuroscientist Giacomo Rizzolatti made a completely accidental yet no less remarkable and groundbreaking discovery about how the brain works. Rizzolatti conducted brain scan experiments on macaque monkeys that involved giving the monkeys a peanut to munch on. Rizzolatti noticed that the neural response of an onlooking monkey in another cage was exactly the same as the monkey actually involved in the experiment. In other words, the neural response of the monkey who was *watching* the eating of the peanut was the same as the response of the monkey who was *actually eating* it.

Intrigued by this accidental discovery, Rizzolatti and his team made further tests and concluded that, as far as the brain is concerned, whether you eat something or just watch something being eaten, they are one and the same neural experience. The brain cannot distinguish between the *actual* sensation of an experience and the *imagined* sensation of the same experience.

Wow! Really? That makes sense. That's why when I see someone else munching a bag of crisps, my mouth starts to water? My brain believes I am actually munching crisps too.

I can feel the saliva forming in my mouth.

Rizzolatti and his team came up with the term *mirror neurons*. As humans, our ability to empathize with other people relies heavily on our ability to mirror the sensations and emotions of others, not least of all so that we can respond to their needs in an appropriate manner. No other animal on the planet manages this level of emotional and empathic intelligence quite as well as human beings. It's one of the characteristics that sets us apart from other mammals and gives us an evolutionary competitive edge.

This uniquely human skill has a distinctive downside, however. Putting myself in someone else's head makes it possible for me to imagine—no, feel, *really* feel—what is going through the mind of a three-year-old child as she descends into the deep end of a swimming pool in Italy, drowning quietly. It also explains why even as I write these words in my home in Norway, I can feel my chest tightening up, my mouth clamming up, and my breathing becoming shallow.

· · ·

"I see this is your first time," the receptionist says to me in a matter-of-fact way. "Come with me, and I'll show you how it works."

Show me how it works? Show me how what works? I ask myself, checking subconsciously that I am still in thought bubble mode, not audible speech bubble mode. I know how *it* works, thank you very much.

She proceeds to a nearby rack of coat hangers from which she pulls out a thin white bathroom robe.

"Change into this."

She then points to a row of white slippers on the floor, the type you might find at the foot of a hotel bed—three star, not five star.

"And take a pair of those."

Then she hands me a plastic cup with a blue lid. The cup is translucent. It's not transparent but translucent. There's a difference. I know that because these were more Latinate words that Titch McCarthy taught me the day he pummeled poor, petrified Peter.

"And you'll need this." She offers no explanation for the cup, and I don't ask for one. "If you can just follow me."

She walks over to a changing room door and gestures for me to go inside and get changed into my sperm sampler costume. Well, she doesn't say *sperm sampler costume*, but that's basically what it is.

A few minutes later, I reappear, now wearing my white bathrobe and my white slippers. I'm not sure they are actually men's slippers, since they are at least a couple of sizes too small and very narrow, which make my extra-wide hobbit feet seem even uglier than they already are. The receptionist then beckons me to follow her toward another row of doors down the hallway.

I try to keep up with her, but the best I can manage in my undersized slippers is a fast shuffle. The linoleum floor has the look and feel of a typical medical center, with its dappled green-gray hue, designed to provide a comfortable, soothing environment and to help the patients relax. What is particular about *this* floor, though, is just *how* smooth and slippery it is under my feet, no doubt due to the many other desperately hopeful men who have shuffled their way across this hallway and buffed the floor up to its current lackluster sheen.

On my way to the doors, I pass another middle-aged man on his way back. He is dressed in the same white robe and miniature slippers, only his gait is somewhat slower and more deliberate than mine—less shuffling, more dragging. He looks forlorn—spent, perhaps? And rosy cheeked. He's looking down at the floor.

The receptionist stops at the second door of four. There is no sign on the door, no "Private" placard or even a "Do Not Disturb" hanging from the handle—just a plain gray office door. You would think that my doctor, with all his window cleaner chirpiness and sense of irony, would have at least hung up a playfully euphemistic "Men at Work" sign on the door or even one that said "Masturbatorium," just to keep things a little more scientific. The only indication that anything is going on inside that room is two lights on the outside: one green, one red.

"Inside, you'll find everything you need to . . ."

Her words hang in the air. There's no need to finish her sentence, in the same way that a postman would ask you to sign for a delivery when he says, "If you could just . . ." It's obvious. All the same, it's too much of a linguistic loose end for me, and I find myself in need of some kind of verbal closure, some kind of syntactic resolution to the half-sentence this receptionist has just uttered.

So, my thought bubbles fill in the blanks for me.

If you could just *finish the job.*

If you could just *jerk off.*

If you could just *stick your cock into this plastic cup while imagining that you are the lead role in a blockbuster porn movie and then fuck it.*

"Remember to lock the door," she tells me. "Then the light outside will turn red, and nobody will disturb you."

As I enter the room, the door behind me closes with a deep, low, reassuring thud, a sound not dissimilar to that of a limousine car door, one that reminds you that you are now safely cocooned in your cockpit of comfort, hidden behind the tinted glass from where you can furtively observe the outside world.

This is no cockpit of comfort, though, and the long fluorescent tube in the middle of the ceiling is about as luxurious and welcoming as the lights of an underground car park. There is a black reclining chair, which may be made of real leather, although when I consider what it is mostly used for, I wonder if imitation leather would be more fitting and practical for the job at hand. Meanwhile, a small TV is perched on top of a bookshelf that contains a selection of magazines, some VHS videos, a VHS player, and—of course—a box of tissues.

I reluctantly slide into the fake leather recliner and reach out for the nearest magazine. This magazine has no features on cars or boats or fishing or hunting. This magazine doesn't have much text in it at all, actually. This magazine has boobs—lots of boobs. And asses. It's porn, but definitely porn of the softer kind. I can see that firing up those mirror neurons I'd been thinking about in the waiting room is going to be a tricky task.

The success of, as well as the pleasure in, masturbation, relies heavily on a person's ability to transport themselves into another world and experience firsthand—no pun intended—the sensations that will bring that person to climax. This is why watching porn can feel so lifelike and why it is so abundantly popular. Porn is a turbocharged ignition of the mirror neuron pathways.

Mirror neurons explain why virtual reality feels so real—because as far as the brain is concerned, it *is* real. By watching other people having unbridled and uncomplicated sex on a screen, my brain transports me into someone else's world, a world where I get to be the lead role in a blockbuster porn movie, a place where I get to vicariously experience what it's like to make love to—or should I say *fuck*, since it *is* a porn movie, after all—what it's like to *fuck* another woman and do it well.

But the most important part of indulging in porn, and what makes porn so difficult to say no to, particularly for men, is that it will help me avoid three important pain points of male vulnerability.

1. The woman I am having sex with won't reject me.

2. The woman I am having sex with won't compare me to anyone else.

3. Arguably the most important of them, she will enjoy it. Loudly.

Oh, yes, once I get my mirror neurons to fire up, I get to be the architect of a domain where my sexual prowess has no limits, a world where I get to shape my sexual fantasies to my precise specifications and needs, a parallel universe where, if only for a short while, I get to be the master of my reality, a *maestro*—a *maestro fuckatore*. Without mirror neurons, this act of sexual self-indulgence would simply not work nearly as well.

But as I begin, I soon realize that this paper version of soft porn is making it more difficult to fire up my mirror neurons than I thought. The dog-eared pages of the magazine suggest that many men before me have come to the same conclusion as they flicked through looking in vain for some kind of inspiration.

Besides, those macaque monkeys in Parma responded best to the *sounds* and *actions* of other monkeys, not images. I need actions. I need sounds. I discard the magazine and turn my attention to the only thing available in this pre-smartphone, pre-Wi-Fi masturbatorium: the VHS video player on the shelf. There are four or five different titles available, all of them from the 1980s and all of them from former Eastern Bloc countries, like Hungary and Bulgaria.

I'll go for Hungarian, I think. *Why not?*

I insert the cassette into the player and press play on the remote. Immediately, the image of a gurning 1980s Hungarian man is thrust into my view. He looks like an Eastern European Tom Selleck, complete with bushy moustache and a seriously hairy chest, and he has just unloaded himself onto the breasts of an expectant Farrah Fawcett lookalike. No warm-up. No story. No foreplay. Straight to the money shot.

Titch McCarthy would have called this kind of scene *in medias res*: a scene that begins in the middle of the action. We had lots of those when we studied Virgil and Homer. Many classic films, such as Martin Scorsese's *Raging Bull*, Quentin Tarantino's *Kill Bill: Volume 2*, and just about every James Bond movie, use this same device. The *in medias res* of this VHS cassette tells me where in the story the last person who watched this got to before he finished.

He didn't even bother to rewind the tape after he was finished.

How inconsiderate of him! Or perhaps he just fell asleep. Maybe he had himself a postcoital nap after filling his plastic cup. But that would have been a bad idea. The receptionist specifically reminded me to bring the sample straight back to her afterward. It was essential not to let the temperature of the semen go below twenty degrees Celsius.

I rewind the tape, lie down on the couch, undo my bathrobe, and settle in for the ride—again, no pun intended. And today I will be riding solo: the Lone Ranger, Hans Solo—or, should I say, Hands Solo?

I'll leave what happened next to your capable imagination, although I *would* like to mention a couple of details.

Detail number one: The video was a kaleidoscope of orgies, a sea of people, a mêlée of arms and legs intertwined into a collage of sexual acts and positions. Perhaps orgies were the in thing in former Communist countries. Communism was, after all, about sharing resources.

Detail number two: There was an inordinate amount of black body hair everywhere: heads, armpits, backs, bottoms, and genitalia. Hair was definitely en vogue in the 1970s and '80s. Donna Summer, Leo Sayer, Michael Jackson (just think of the album cover for *The Wall*), Diana Ross, Ali MacGraw, Frank Zappa, Brian May (who has worn his seventies haircut ever since, actually), and, of course, Tom Selleck and Farrah Fawcett.

The combination of the hairy limbs and the cacophony of porn actors moaning in sexual delight prove to be somewhat of a challenge for my mirror neurons. The last place I can imagine wanting to transport myself right now is a 1970s orgy where I am surrounded by a sea of hirsute Hungarians.

Finally, after much concentration and sheer brute-force determination, I manage to finish the task at hand. *Masturbationem perfectus.* Mission accomplished. Or, as Julius Caesar might have said, "Veni, vidi, *veni!*" I came, I saw, I came.

I carefully place the blue lid back on to the translucent plastic cup and examine my donation. There is not much to show for all my efforts—hardly more than a blob of the good stuff. How utterly disappointing! *I've blown more snot than this into a handkerchief on a cold January morning,* I think. I wonder if it matters how much one produces.

Quality, not quantity, I say to myself. But what if it's quality *and* quantity? The doctor did tell me to "save myself" for five days before coming in. The gurning Hungarian with the Tom Selleck moustache produced *lots* more than this when he finished on the Farrah Fawcett lookalike. No time to worry about that now. I have to get it back to the receptionist. I open the door again and make my way toward her.

It is at this point that I understand why the man I passed in the hallway appeared so forlorn and flustered. I am now keenly aware that anyone not currently wearing a white bathrobe and slippers—which means nearly everybody—must be very conscious of what I've just been doing.

I can sense that my cheeks are flushed too, which, along with the pumped-up veins on my forearms, announce to all around exactly what I've been up to for the past fifteen minutes:

conducting experiments in the masturbatorium. Wanking. Tossing off. Choking the chicken. Beating the bishop. Strangling the Cyclops. Slamming the salami. Indulging in hand-to-*gland* combat. And there is absolutely nothing wrong with any of those pleasurable pastimes, despite what my Catholic teachers at St. Brendan's would have had me believe, so why should I be embarrassed? I shouldn't be.

I am, though—shamefully, painfully embarrassed. That man I'd passed on my way to my room was doing his walk of shame. Now, it was my turn.

I'd given urine samples before and blood samples. Even stool samples. But there was something different about providing a sperm sample. Sperm is what makes men essentially men. This male reproductive cell is one of the few things that distinguishes men from women, just like ovaries distinguish women from men. Sperm provides men with a role and a purpose in nature's grand design, a competitive edge in an evolutionary marketplace where it has become increasingly difficult and frustrating to prove one's worth. Sperm is what men do—or don't do, as is my case. Hence the sense of inadequacy, the sense of shame.

It doesn't take long for the results of my sperm analysis to come back from the lab, and a few days later, I am back in the consultation room.

I had produced 485 million little swimmers. Well, I say "swimmers," but only 64 percent of them actually swam, of which no more than 32 percent swam quickly. *Still, that's over 150 million fast swimmers, I think. That's pretty good odds.*

However, of the 485 million sperm I delivered in my plastic cup, only 4 percent had what was referred to as a "normal appearance." Still, that's almost 20 million normal sperm. What the fuck? I am back at the fairground at the shoot-the-duck stall, with my twenty million shots. Surely I could hit a duck before I run out of bullets! The doctor's conclusion is clear and unequivocal, though, and it is written in bold letters on my sperm report.

"Sperm quality: Very poor. Fertilization is possible, but likelihood is low."

It's a blow, a real blow. I'd never thought about it before it actually happened. I'd never even considered that I could not make a woman pregnant. In fact, many a time, in my former days as a wild, carefree, irresponsible, oat-sowing young man, when my head and loins would be brimming with testosterone, I would have the opposite problem, worrying if I had made my latest bed companion pregnant. I don't think I am the only guy in the world who has quietly and secretly waited anxiously to see if his latest fling would call to let him know that there had been a little accident.

An accident, for heaven's sake. We actually called it an accident when we unintentionally got someone pregnant—not a miracle of life, not a wonder of Mother Nature. No. An accident.

Right now, as I read my report, I begin to realize that I won't be causing any accidents, not even if I am driving the wrong way down a one-way fallopian tube. This blow is like a left hook that sends me spiraling down toward the canvas. I truly don't know if I'll make it back up for the count.

CHAPTER 10

Rubbing Salt in the Wounds

I feel triumphant on the bus ride home after Derek's palm thrashing, although I must admit that I am grateful I am not biking home. I'm not sure I could have held on to the handlebars very well.

As I enter the kitchen, school bag still drooped over my left shoulder, both hands throbbing, my father looks up and greets me with a fiercely ironic, "Fuck me! His Royal Highness has arrived!"

"Sorry I'm late," I reply. "The bus was late."

"Is it okay if we eat now, Your Grace?" My father's words ooze sarcasm and scorn.

I say nothing. I know when it is best to say nothing. Just like the early hours of that same morning when we passed each other in the kitchen. No need to douse the pilot light with fuel, right?

I sit down at the table across from my father and sister, and my mother places three steaming plates of pasta in front of us: one for me, one for my sister, and one for my father. Just one plate is missing—my mother's. She is still dishing out her own plate. She always serves herself last.

While she is still at the stove, my father tucks in, shoveling a heaping mound of spaghetti into his mouth. Then, he drops his fork noisily onto the plate. "How much salt did you put in the sauce?"

I can hear my father's anger in the tone of the question. From across the dinner table, I can smell it on his breath, which has the unmistakable stench of a man who recently awoke from an unsatisfying slumber.

He's been working the night shift this week, just as he does every third week. He's on a three-shift rotation at the factory. One week of early mornings from six a.m. until two p.m. The next week from two p.m. until ten p.m. The third week from ten at night until six in the morning: the night shift. He's been on this three-shift treadmill for the past six years. It's tough—really tough. But the night shifts are the toughest. The night shifts really take their toll. They wear him down. They piss him off. They make him focus on the insignificant microdetails of his life and turn them into macroanalogies of everything that's wrong with the world. Today's microdetail is salt. And unless we can do something to avert him, the person on the receiving end of his macroanalogy will be my mother.

Salt. From the Latin *sal*. The word salary comes from the same Latin root. When soldiers in Ancient Rome could not be paid in coins, they were sometimes paid in salt instead, such was its validity as a currency as well as its importance as a basic, yet essential, mineral. Wars have even been fought over salt. The Austrian city of Salzburg means "The Salt Castle," a testimony to the fact that its fortune was built on the "white gold" of the time. Christopher Columbus's voyage was said to have been partly financed by the production of salt in the south of Spain.

Salt has literally seasoned, preserved, and enriched the lives of millions of people all over the world, rich and poor. Of all the condiments in a kitchen, there is nothing more basic, more essential, and—crucially—more affordable than a bag of salt. No matter how poor Vincenzo felt on his measly chocolate factory salary, he could always afford to buy a bag of salt—with fancy wrapping and all. The day he couldn't afford to go a little crazy on the salt would be the day he might as well just stick his shotgun under his chin and pull the trigger.

"Did you hear me, woman? I asked how much fucking salt you put in the sauce."

The extra swear word in his question is a dead giveaway that his level of irritation has just gone up a notch. My mother ignores the provocation. She takes her plate of pasta and sits down at the table. This isn't the first time she's heard this kind of question or comment from my father at dinnertime. The comments always come when he is in a bad mood. If it isn't the amount of salt in his sauce, it might be how long she cooked the pasta or whether she forgot to put oregano in the meatballs or how long she soaked the dried *fagioli*. Didn't she know that she had to soak them for at least eight hours? Otherwise, they will end up being too hard.

Under normal circumstances, she would have answered back by now. My father is, after all, criticizing her cooking skills, and in her world—as well as in her words—"you don't fuck with a woman's cooking." She doesn't tell him how to do his job or how to fix his car, so why should he tell her how to do her cooking? My mother could give as much as she took from my father. She knows how to stick up for herself.

Sure, in public, my mother was often the doting spouse whose role was to promote her husband's image as the head of the family, to cover his ass, to make him look less of an incompetent, like when he melted his suitcase of chocolates. This, she did with great skill and aplomb. She also did it with remarkable grace. But once inside the privacy of the family home, my mother had her specific areas and domains where she ruled supreme.

My mother was tough, too—tough as coffin nails. This image of Italian mothers doting on each and every whim of their children, especially their sons, is a somewhat incomplete and unnuanced picture, especially mothers of the backwater south of Italy.

I recall my father's sister, Auntie Filomena, who also moved away from Forino to one of the snobbiest cities of the prosperous industrial north, Parma, a city that is referred to by Italians as *Piccola Parigi*, or "Little Paris." Unimpressed by her bourgeoisie milieu, Auntie Filomena remained true to her humble, unpretentious roots. "You can take Filomena out of Forino, but you can't take Forino out of Filomena," she would say. For instance, she refused to modify her unmistakably southern name to a more acceptable northern version, like Filly, or Fil, or Mena, as so many other migrants did, all of them keen to assimilate with their more urbane northern citizens. So it seemed logical that Filomena never stopped speaking her southern Irpinian dialect, either. I loved that about her.

Filomena also knew how to play the doting wife up to a certain point but would never shy from putting her husband in his place when required. She was never afraid to call a spade a spade, often doing so with some rather colorful language more fitting of a trooper than a lady. Auntie Filomena didn't just call a spade a spade—she called a spade a *fucking* spade! In many ways, Auntie Filomena was my father in a skirt!

My mother belonged to the same breed of unapologetic, hardened, resilient women who could dish out punishment as easily and freely as she could dish out a *ragù alla Bolognese* and often with the same utensil too—a wooden spoon.

Once, during a particularly savage beating she gave me after I'd managed to break one of her kitchen drawers by lying down in it and pretending it was a bed, she actually broke the wooden spoon on my skull. And then she beat me even more for making her break her spoon on my head! I know! How fucked up is that?

My mother would normally have answered back, told my father that he was imagining things, that he was tired, that too much salt would be the death of him, to shut the fuck up—whatever. But not today. Today, she senses that something is amiss. Something is not right.

"I asked you how much fucking salt did you put in the sauce? Are you scrimping on the goddamn salt again?"

As I sit there and sense the same impending danger as my mother, I can't help feeling responsible for the negative atmosphere in the room. It was me who delayed dinner this evening. It was me who kept them all waiting for me to come home from school. It wasn't unusual for me to be the last to arrive home because of the hour-long bus journey. However, on this particular day, I'd arrived even later than normal. My father was already hungry, tired, irritable. He was a hair-triggered mousetrap waiting for a feather to fall and set him off. Of all the days to come home late from school, this is not the day to do that. And all because of a chemistry exam.

But he didn't really care about the food. These questions have one sole purpose—to provoke a reaction, to goad my mother into an argument, which will then turn into a fight.

Psychologists and sociologists call it *aggression displacement*. A beta baboon loses a fight to an alpha baboon. This is humiliating for the beta, especially in front of so many other baboons. So what does he do about it? He finds the omega baboon and starts a fight with him, a fight he knows he will win. This victory makes him feel much better about himself.

It's the same in the human world. Display aggression or violence with someone you know cannot fight back or you know will lose, and it provides enormous relief from whatever pain or humiliation you may be feeling. This is why whenever unemployment rates rise among male populations, rates of domestic violence go up too. Whenever there is a downturn in the economy, spousal and child abuse skyrocket. Even when a man's football team loses on a Saturday afternoon, expect there to be a spike in domestic violence in that football team's town. As we start to eat our pasta, we can sense that we are about to become part of those frightful statistics.

My father doesn't care about the salt; that's just an excuse. It is the same amount as the day before, and he'd said nothing then. My mother knows it is the same amount because she only used half of the sauce from the bottle. Not only that, but the sauce came from the same batch of tomato sauce bottles that her family made that very same summer in Italy. It was the same sauce they'd made every year since she could remember—hundreds of kilos of San Marzano plum tomatoes, gently boiled in huge saucepans, pressed and pulped and poured into glass bottles. What changed was not the taste but the person tasting it.

Normally, my mother knew when to pick her battles. Today, though, she was about to get it wrong—very wrong.

"It's the same sauce as yesterday. So if you liked it yesterday, then you should fucking well like it today too," she replies.

Oh, no, Mamma, you just took the bait! Why did you take the bait?

"Are you calling me a liar?" My father's focus has shifted from the salt to her now.

"You call yourself what you like," my mother replies. "All I can tell you is the facts. The truth. You can see what you like."

And with that, she stands up and walks away from the dinner table and sits down on the sofa in the living room. She is no more than a few feet away from the dinner table, but the symbolic distance is far greater.

Silence fills the kitchen. It is the silence before the tsunami, when the animals have long since understood what is about to happen, when they have already sought refuge on higher ground, leaving mothers, fathers, and children to their complacent ignorance. It is the silence of the Himalayan night that engulfs the solitary, frostbitten mountain climber who knows that his fellow climbers have no choice but to wait until dawn to send out a search party, when, surely, it will be too late. It is the silence of a child drowning quietly in a swimming pool.

The silence is broken momentarily by my father's invitation to us—my sister and me—to start our meals, although the underlying disdain and irritability in his voice makes his words sound more like an order than an invitation: "What are you waiting for? Start eating."

Today's choice of pasta is spaghetti—Barilla's famous spaghetti No. 5, to be precise. My father insists that the normal spaghetti is too thin and tends to get overcooked. No. 5 is slightly thicker. More to get your teeth into, he says.

It's been a couple of hours since Derek's flagellation, and those purple streaks across my palms have started to swell up. I am not sure if they will blister. Perhaps. And it's too late to run them under a cold tap now. My swollen, pulsating palms make it almost impossible for me to twirl my spaghetti. I struggle to get the proper grip around the fork, a delicate, three-fingered grip that requires you to crease your palm. I try it once, and a sharp burning sensation shoots down my forearm. I flinch. I try again, barely managing to smother a hiss of pain over the same burning sensation. Perhaps if I go easy on the creasing of my palms, that might help. But all that does is turn my three-fingered precision grip into the four-fingered grope of a clumsy primate trying to rotate a Rubik's cube. Instead of a tidy, ball-shaped nest of pasta, I end up with blob of tomato-drenched tumbleweed that I hurriedly stuff into my mouth. The inevitable splattering of sauce and squelching of cheeks as I suck the long strings of spaghetti into my gob is a lighthouse for my father's anger.

"What the fuck?" he shouts. "I said you can start *eating* your pasta, not *hoovering* your pasta! You sound like a fucking Englishman!"

My second attempt is markedly better, no doubt because my father is glaring at me, watching my every move.

"That's better," my father says. "Shall I put some more salt on your pasta for you?"

Fuck! What do I say now? If I say yes, I will be taking his side. That would make him right and my mother wrong. And she's *not* wrong. This is not like pretending that someone's homemade wine tastes as good a DOCG wine. This is a completely different dilemma.

Then again, by saying yes to him now, I avoid escalating the conflict. But she's not wrong! *He* is wrong. And not just about the pasta, either. He is wrong to be treating her like this. She helped him separate all those chocolates, for God's sake. She loves him. Why would you want to fight someone who you know loves you? The sauce tastes fine. In fact, it tastes great, just like all the other pasta sauces we've eaten this year.

"Uh . . . I'm okay, Papà. I think . . . uhm . . . it tastes fine to me."

"Another twat who knows fuck all about fuck all!"

My father's swear rate has gone up: two fucks and a twat in a nine-word sentence—a ratio of three to one. That is not good. And the strength of his logic has gone markedly down too. I am pretty sure that if he'd been part of one of our balloon debate sessions at St. Brendan's, his counterargument "another twat who knows fuck all about fuck all" would not have won him many votes among the jury of teachers and fellow students.

And when he swears, he does it in his native Irpinia dialect—Irpino—which makes it sound all the more ferocious and menacing. Irpino is a subdialect of Neapolitan and does not have that happy-go-lucky, singsong rhythm and tone of what most people understand to be Italian. An English friend of mine once described Irpino as sounding a bit like "a dog barking in Arabic!" My father is about to go on a rant of biblical proportions, the kind Quentin Tarantino would have been proud of.

"Why the fuck do I bother sending you to school? To learn about Latin? What good is that anyway? Nobody speaks Latin anymore! When are they going to teach you something useful, like how much salt you need in your sauce? Sometimes I even wonder if you know that your cock is not just for pissing out of! What the hell did I move to this fucking country for? Why in the Pope's name do I bother going to work? To turn you and your mother into ignorant twats who know fuck all about fuck all? Why the . . . ?"

But before he can finish his Tarantinian monologue, my mother cuts him down with three fateful, Irpino words.

"Ma quanne mor?" (When are you going to die?)

Every time I visualize what happened next, it happens in slow motion, even though, in reality, it couldn't have taken more than twenty seconds—thirty, max.

With his left hand, my father flips up his plate from the table. His right hand slides effortlessly underneath the plate, which is still hot from the freshly served pasta—not as hot as when Om grasped the glowing tap in chemistry class but certainly as hot, if not hotter, than when Derek strafed my palms that very same day. In one smooth movement, his right arm rises above his head, his wrists rotate to position the steaming plate of pasta at an angle of approximately forty-five degrees, he leans out of his chair, placing his weight onto his front leg. He looks like a discus thrower from ancient Greece, about to unleash his power, about to launch his discus high into the air. And then he launches. But not *up* into the air—down. One stride forward, one arm crashing down, one slam dunk—bull's-eye. He throws the hot pasta and the plate it sat on straight into the side of my mother's face as she sits on the sofa.

There is an explosion of blood—blood everywhere. But it is too red to be blood. It is San Marzano sauce. Meatballs are strewn all over the floor. Spaghetti lands as far away as the foot of the television stand in the other corner of the living room. And there is blood on the walls. No, that is sauce too. At least it's easier to wash off than blood, but that sauce will be a bugger to get out of the carpet. And it will smell, too, for weeks.

And the noise. My God, the noise! Ceramic meeting cheekbone. Sixty to nought in point one of a second. Instant and total transfer of energy from an inanimate moving object to an inanimate stationary object. And now she is screaming, really screaming, like a lamb being slaughtered for the feast.

He's grabbed her by the hair and pulled her down on to the floor, and now he is dragging her across the floor by her big beehive hair. She was always behind the times, fashion-wise. "Beehives were in during the sixties, Mamma," we would say, but she looked great with a beehive, even if it was retro.

There is blood on his hands. My father has blood on his hands. No, it is sauce. *There's fucking sauce everywhere, for fuck's sake!*

Now she is on the floor next to me, at my feet, looking up at me, screaming. I can't make out her words. There are no words. Lambs being slaughtered don't speak; they barely manage to scream.

She is still moving, still being dragged like a plow through clay. I can read her eyes. She is begging me to help her—fucking *begging* me.

But I can't move. I am stuck to my chair. Fight, flight, or freeze; I freeze. My whole body is frozen like a statue, except for my hands, which are still throbbing from Derek's beating. And even if I could move, *cui bono*—what good is it for? What good am I at that moment? I can barely twirl my spaghetti fork, let alone defend my mother. What good am I for? I am twelve years old, and I cannot save my mother. *Cui bono*, Titch McCarthy? *Cui bono?*

But she is gone anyway, dragged past me toward the kitchen, still screaming. And now they are in the kitchen, his left hand still clenched around her beehive hairdo. His right hand pulls open the cutlery drawer and frantically scours the inside for something.

Now he has a knife in his hand—a fucking knife! Like a lamb to slaughter—a lamb with a black beehive.

Papà, no. Papà no.

He studies the knife, a six-inch vegetable knife, as if he is checking that he's selected the right size for the task at hand. He appears confused, disappointed even. He throws it back into the drawer and, instead, pulls out something longer—a twelve-inch wooden spoon. I bet she wishes she'd snapped *that* one on my skull. He thrusts the spoon into the sauce, jerks her head up, and smears the sauce on her mouth.

"Are you sure you didn't put too much salt in the fucking sauce?"

Oh, Mamma. Do you still think that life is beautiful even when it's ugly?

CHAPTER 11

Sooner or Later, One Way or Another

"Don't look so glum. This report is actually very useful." The doctor is upbeat. In his line of work, I guess he has to be.

But I'm still thinking about the phrase *Sperm quality: very poor*. "How the bloody hell is this useful, Doc?"

After explaining that finding out why couples don't get pregnant is a process of elimination, the doctor says he has an idea—a theory, he calls it. It's quite a common procedure, nothing to be alarmed about, he reassures me. I already don't believe him when he says these words.

"What I think has happened is that your epididymis may have gotten itself a little kink."

"What's an epididymis?"

"It's the tightly coiled tube that connects your testicle to the rest of your reproductive system. It basically transports your sperm and gets it ready for ejaculation."

"And what do you mean by kink?"

"I think this tube has been dented or twisted, which means that the sperm is getting held up, getting stuck there. It's a bit like having a blockage in the U-bend under your kitchen sink. I don't know if you've ever had to open up one of those U-bends and clean out the crap at the bottom? It's pretty rancid."

On my previous visit, the doctor's plumbing euphemism had annoyed me, but this time it creates a vivid image of the underbelly of a kitchen sink and a hundred million sperm drowning in their own ejaculate—a hundred million potential Olivias unable to hold their breath any longer.

"So, what do you suggest, Doc? Are you going to clean out my tubes? Are you going to make me drink shitloads of vinegar and baking soda?"

"No, no, nothing like that. I just need to straighten them out a bit. Untwist them so that they don't get stuck there, and so that they can swim on in their merry way toward your wife's ovaries."

"And how are you going to straighten them out?" I ask nervously.

"Well, I need to go in there and feel where the kink is and straighten it out. Untwist it. It's quite straightforward, really."

"Yeah, for you maybe!"

I wonder whether the doctor has ever had a twelve-inch prong stuck up *his* arse or whether he's had his epididymis straightened out. I also wonder whether his mirror neurons are actually firing correctly, since he shows little if any empathy toward me when he performs those acts on me.

The next thing I know, I'm lying on that examination table

again, in the fetal position, staring at the same posters on the wall that I'd stared at the first time I'd visited the clinic.

Symphysis pubis. Corpus cavernosum. Corpus spongiosum. Penile urethra. Scrotum. Testis, prostate, anus, rectum. *Oh, fuck! Here we go agaiiiiinnnnnnnnn!*

He's inside again, realigning my testicles, massaging and unraveling my sperm tubes, like you would unravel a yoyo before you reel it in on its string. He has redefined the expression "up close and personal."

"Done!" he exclaims triumphantly as he snaps off his surgical gloves and I am left to clean up the mess again.

"Just make sure you keep them little swimmers moving. No traffic jams in there, okay?"

"What? Sorry? What do you mean by keep them moving?"

"Make sure you ejaculate frequently and regularly."

"I travel a lot with my work, Doctor. Sometimes I can be away a whole week in another continent."

"Well, I'm sure you can think of a way to solve that problem. You can't have them getting held up in your tubes anymore."

I manage a feeble smile as I realize that the doctor has just given me permission to masturbate on a daily basis. I want to ask him for a doctor's note so that I can show it to my boss at work.

Patient requires ten minutes, twice a day, to retire to a suitable masturbatorium to ejaculate.

Now *that* would be something!

Those visits to the Andrology Centre were the most bizarre,

the most invasive, and the scariest encounters with the medical profession in my life. They were also enlightening—in good and bad ways.

It was the last time anyone stuck their finger up my rectum, although, like any other middle-aged man, I probably have a few prostate examinations to look forward to. No rush, though, I think as I hobble and wobble toward the car park like a Galápagos penguin who's been basking in the Pacific sun a little too long and seeks refreshment in the chilly surf.

Once inside my car, I pull the door shut, the *thunk* telling me I am in a place of tranquility and security, a place of humble reflection and privacy. Right now, I think it's the privacy I most appreciate. Right now, nobody knows where I am or what I am doing, and it feels reassuring. I can be alone to lick the wounds of this latest emasculating ordeal. I can be alone with my thoughts, my sense of injured pride, and my oversensitive epididymis. I slide the gear lever into drive and head home, naïvely believing that I am good to go, that the worst is over in my journey toward parenthood, that I have been stamped with the Ducal Crown of Andrological Excellence.

But nothing could be further from the truth. Olivia at this point is not even so much as a twinkle in her Daddy's eye. At this point, Olivia is ten years away. A brother and a sister will enter the world before her. Right now, I don't know that though.

All I know is that I am feeling less and less of a man. I also know that I am drifting away from my wife. We don't really talk about it from an emotional perspective. At least I don't. I don't know how to. I have so much that I want to say but it all involves admitting that I feel inadequate, and lonely, and vulnerable. I don't know how to do that. I would rather drown quietly in my sea of shame and self-reproach.

What I do know how to do, though, is grin and bear it. Flex my muscles and parade my invulnerability. My resilience. My mental stamina. We men are so good at providing a positive spin on our weaknesses and shortcomings. But none of my façade of fortitude will prepare me for the many, *many* heartaches and disappointments that await me.

. . .

It's a Monday afternoon, and I'm at the IVF clinic in Oslo. I am looking through a microscope, and the thing that I am staring at through the eyepiece reminds me of a single cherry blossom flower.

I think, *It's way too early in the year for cherry blossoms in Oslo.*

The flower is my daughter, an eight-cell embryo. Not many fathers can say they have seen their daughter three days after conception, but that's exactly what I am looking at now, and it is truly an awe-inspiring sight—so delicate, so fragile.

David Fairchild, the American botanist who brought cherry blossoms to the United States, once wrote, "A small microscope will reveal wonders a thousand times more thrilling than anything which Alice saw behind the looking glass."[1] He was so right. And

---

1   David Fairchild, *The World Was My Garden: Travels of a Plant Explorer* (New York: Charles Scribner's Sons, 1939), 11.

if anyone knew how to introduce new life into a new environment, then it was him.

The embryo's name will be Emily. She will be Olivia's big sister. Before Emily came her brother, Christian. I saw him under a microscope too. Both Christian and Emily are remarkable children, living proof not only of the marvels of modern science but also of the miracle and mystery of life itself. When Christian was born, I wept like I'd never wept before. After all we'd been through to get there, to finally hold a living, breathing soul in my hands brought with it more emotions than any man could—or *should*, for that matter—keep inside him. I guess the fact that Christian was our firstborn made the occasion extra special. You know the old adage "There's only one first impression"; well, there's only one firstborn, too.

But there was something even more remarkable about Emily. Perhaps it was because I was seeing her in her eight-cell embryo state. When I saw Christian, he was a sixteen-cell embryo—twice Emily's "age." I smile to myself.

Normal parents don't get to see their children at such an early stage in their lives; only parents who go through IVF—*in vitro fertilization*—do. That's where Emily is right now: *in vitro*, in a glass. You were right, Titch McCarthy, Latin really is alive and well. She's in a glass petri dish, just centimeters from my eyeball, all eight cells of her. Emily is a microscopic translucent miracle.

At this precise moment, I am praying that Emily is as alive and well as the Latin that Titch taught us at school. I remember I had to pray twice for Christian for each round of IVF. The first time I prayed for him, my prayers went unanswered.

Before these eight cells can become Emily, they have to divide into sixteen cells, then thirty-two, sixty-four, and so on, until she becomes what the doctors at the IVF clinic have told us is called a *blastocyst*. What an ugly-sounding name for such a miracle. It sounds like a swear word. Piss off, you bloody blastocyst! That's exactly what Christian version 1.0 ended up being: a bloody blastocyst, deemed by Mother Nature to be substandard and therefore rejected. But my wife and I tried again, and on the second round of IVF, Christian version 2.0 became our firstborn child.

When I observe Emily today, a healthy teenager, standing tall and proud in her mane of golden Nordic hair, I can only marvel at the fact that I saw her when she was just eight cells. She was one of an original batch of eight eggs that her mother produced. Of the original eight, only three survived the first three critical days in the petri dish. Of those three, the doctors said that only one looked healthy enough to make it all the way through a nine-month pregnancy. That was Emily. Perhaps that's why Emily's birth was even more remarkable than the first. Emily is a fighter.

The standard procedure was to put two embryos back into the mother's uterus, even if only one looked healthy enough. Just in case. Of course, that also meant that both embryos could, in theory, survive and make it to babyhood. This is why so many IVF parents end up having twins. Whenever I see older parents with young twins, I can't help wondering if they went through IVF too. I also can't help imagining the husband in a masturbatorium.

They put two embryos back into my wife's womb. The doctor didn't waste any time preparing us for the most likely outcome.

One baby if we're lucky, he told us. He didn't use those exact words, of course, but we knew what he meant. This was, after all, our third round of IVF, and we were becoming quite knowledgeable about the whole process, including the most important aspect, which was that doctors can't guarantee pregnancy. They can only help.

The role of IVF doctors is to assist, to tinker with nature and *play* God, but they are not *actually* God. They can only provide a helping hand. Assisted reproductive technology is the official term they use, or ART for short. And it really is as much an art as it is a science to these IVF specialists. Like medical Edvard Munchs, they have an idea of what the final result will look like. They may even play around with slightly different styles and techniques, but there is no guarantee that it will actually work. And even if it does work, they don't know exactly how they will get there, or how long it will take.

What the doctors do know is that, statistically speaking, the longer they work at the art, the more likely they are to succeed. As one female doctor reassuringly put it to my tearful wife after our first round of IVF, "Sooner or later, one way or another, the vast majority of women who want to get pregnant do get pregnant."

Comforting words. But she left out the tail end of her sentence: "But you might be as mad as Edvard Munch himself by the time you get there!"

That's exactly how IVF makes you feel, right up to the point when you actually succeed and hold a healthy child in your arms. IVF is a process that gnaws at your sense of sanity. Day after day, you hope and you pray. By the end, when you do succeed—*even if* you succeed, I would say—you are left in a state of intense emotional fragility and a generally frayed state of mind.

Even today, I can still feel the dull thud of disappointment in my chest when I recollect the image of my wife walking out of the bathroom, negative pregnancy test in hand, her face shrouded in sadness and despondency. I remember how we embraced, how we held each other's grief as best we could. And grief it was—heavy, unrelenting grief. It was our first official death in the family, only there would be no actual body to grieve over, no visit to the morgue. There was no funeral, no flowers, no heartfelt eulogy, no brass coffin handle to hold on to tightly, no gravestone to mark a final resting place.

I remember how we tried to talk our way up and out of the gloom of this bereavement by telling each other that it was normal not to succeed the first time. We even consulted our special IVF info-pack, the one the clinic had given us with all the national statistics on first-time IVF pregnancies.

I remember so well how we consoled each other with data that clearly indicated that fewer than a third of the couples were successful on their first attempt. The odds went up for every time we tried, we assured each other. We just needed to keep trying.

"Sooner or later, one way or another, the vast majority of women who want to get pregnant do get pregnant."

I also remember how I took it on myself to be the one who showed strength in this time of emotional pain and sorrow. I would be the one to pull us through this crisis. I would be the strong one, the tough one. I would be the man, because that's what men do, right?

So it would be my strength and national statistics that would get us through this, that would strengthen the bond between my wife and me. Thinking back on it all now, I realize how ridiculous a strategy this was. Instead of falling into each other's bottomless pit of grief and being there for each other—just being there—fragile and vulnerable, my emotional autopilot override instructed me to go into macho mode.

The problem was that initially our strategy helped, at least a bit. But once I found myself alone with my own thoughts, I couldn't escape the same niggling, gnawing sensation inside of me. It was *me* who had failed to deliver. It was me who had failed to hold up my side of the bargain. We had a pact, my wife and me, an agreement, a carnal concord to make a child together, and I had welched. My seeds of life had failed. I'd had half a doctor's hand up my anal tract to untwist my epididymis. I'd meticulously followed the doctor's orders to "keep them moving" and keep them fresh—all to no avail. My seeds were simply not a catalyst for life.

"It takes two to tango," a friend of mine had quipped, trying to comfort me.

"That may be true," I replied, "but right now it feels like I am tangoing with two left feet."

My wife had had tests too, tons of them. She'd had numerous visits to the gynecologist, Pap smear tests, vaginal examinations, hormone treatments, and fertility drugs. And then there were the copious amounts of estrogen-blocking drugs that had tricked her hypothalamus and pituitary gland into releasing excessive quantities of hormones into her bloodstream, so that her ovaries would produce as many eggs as humanly possible. Instead of the normal one mature egg, these drugs forced her to spawn as many as twenty at a time! In none of these tests were there any indications that she was anything but fully equipped to make, bear, and deliver a child.

As always, my wife bore her responsibility and burden without so much as a whisper of complaint. While I was whinging and whining about a little bit of epididymis fiddling, not once did my wife complain about having foreign objects and human fingers inserted into her various cavities. She remained stoic throughout, the kind of stoicism that Nordics often excel at, no doubt a genetic by-product of the generations before them who'd had to survive adverse climes. Not once did she flinch when the needles injected drugs into her veins. Not once did she doubt the importance of the task at hand. She was silent, stoic, and serene.

Her entire selflessness was all the more noteworthy and admirable, since she must have realized eventually that *she* wasn't the problem. And still she carried on. By the time the doctors were ready to do the first round of assisted fertilization, my wife had been to hormonal hell and back. All that remained was to "introduce" the father's seed to the eggs.

This they did, literally. They introduced a bunch of my sperm cells to one of my wife's eggs. All those swimmers had to do was swim across the petri dish over to the egg and fertilize it. All that egg required was for one (just one!) of the two million sperm cells to swim over, whisper, "Well, hello there, honey" into the egg's ear, and—boom!—one pregnant woman.

They couldn't even manage that. Instead, they swam around aimlessly, like goldfish in a pond, until they ran out of steam and died.

The doctors moved swiftly on to plan B: ICSI—intracytoplasmic sperm injection. This is where they forcibly inject one seed into an egg and hope that nature will do the rest. No introductions, no chat-up lines, no embarrassing silences or rejections from the egg. It is the equivalent of a shotgun wedding in the sperm-egg world. It's less *assisted* fertilization and more *enforced* fertilization. That didn't work either.

My wife had become a walking, spawning laboratory of unexplained and involuntary childlessness, a constant reminder that I was incomplete as a man. I was incompetent, not functioning properly, an out-of-order vending machine that wouldn't spit out the items she'd paid for. Unexplained infertility? It wasn't so unexplainable to me. It was pretty clear to me who the culprit was. Me.

That's when the doubts began getting real traction in my mind about whether we were even meant to be a couple in the first place. One thought in particular would dominate my internal dialogue—that this was nature's way of saying we were incompatible. If we refused to take nature's hint, we would end up childless and alone, bitter and resentful of each other. The thought would not go away. That seed of doubt took root in my brain and began to sprout, spreading and festering like a malignant, life-destroying tumor, eroding away any remnant of sanity.

The doctors told us to not give up. Keep trying, they said. "Sooner or later, one way or another, the vast majority of women who want to get pregnant do get pregnant." But they never said who all these women would get pregnant *with*.

We picked ourselves up and carried on trying—every month, for months on end.

This is when I discovered that lovemaking and babymaking are not necessarily the same thing. *Love*making was fun. It was flippant. It was free. It was pleasurable. *Baby*making, though— that was very different. That was mechanical. It was calculated, predictable, and predetermined.

CHAPTER 12

Diamonds Are a Man's Best Fiend

There are a variety of indications that a woman is ovulating. First, the woman starts to produce cervical mucus. It is fairly impossible for the man to know when that happens. But there is another sign that a woman is ovulating, which is much more perceptible to a man. Her voice. By a remarkable quirk of nature, whenever a woman starts to ovulate, the pitch of her voice goes up. Yes, that's right. Research has shown that a women's voice can go up 15.6 hertz. That's half a semitone. This change in pitch makes the woman sound more feminine and more fertile to the man. It signals to her mate that she is ready. It's a subtle but significant change, one that only the male partner will notice. And when he does notice it, the feeling will be so subliminal that he may not even consciously register it. All he will know is that he will feel a little extra horny.

It's very different in the animal world. Female baboons, for example, when they are ovulating, their butts turn bright red. In the baboon world, *everyone* can see when a female is ovulating.

That wouldn't work at all in the human world. I mean, imagine how difficult it would be for a woman to go to a beach around ovulation time. And women's sports events like the ladies' tennis tournament at Wimbledon would face some significant scheduling challenges. Can you imagine how that would look on TV as a player bends down to receive a serve? Women football players would have to wear extra-large shorts to hide their glowing red butts, unless they played for Liverpool or Bayern Munich, that is.

Then there is the woman's basal body temperature, which goes up about a half a degree Celsius during ovulation. Whenever I saw a thermometer appear in our apartment, whether it was in the bathroom or the bedside table, I knew my wife's basal body temperature was about to change and that it was almost time.

Whenever I heard my wife's voice go up a semitone, I knew that I would soon be summoned to do my duty. I knew that my services would soon be required. Just sit tight and wait for the call. And she would come up to me, thermometer in hand, and hiss in my ear, "It's time!"

That hiss was about as sexually arousing as a slow tire puncture. And it made absolutely no difference that the hiss was half a semitone higher than normal. There are fewer things in the world that will snuff out a man's libido than having to perform on demand.

Perhaps if my wife had been a hyena, then that would have worked better since, in the hyena world, the females are the dominant ones in the pack. Not only are they dominant, but when they intimidate the male hyena, he shows his deference and submission toward the female by getting an erection. While most animals and humans bow their heads or lower their gaze toward their superiors, male hyenas actually get a stiffy! The bigger the erection, the more submissive the male.

But I am no hyena. And neither am I a Pavlovian dog. You can tinkle that bell as much as you like, you can hiss dulcet semitones in my ear, but the only response it will trigger in me is paralyzing stage fright, combined with a blood-draining sense of shame and inadequacy. And blood-draining *anything* is not what a man needs just before his mad, mechanical lovemaking.

The end result is something all men dread will happen to them. My soldier would not stand to attention. If there is one ailment, one disorder, one malady that will plague a man like no other, one source of vulnerability that bedevils any man who has walked this planet, regardless of his age, race, or religion, then it is the dreaded erectile dysfunction—when that soldier won't stand to attention, when the pocket rocket won't launch, when the fun gun won't fire.

If you happen to be one of those men who can just perform on demand, then congratulations—and fuck off! For the rest of us lesser mortals, the mental anguish and psychological pain of this most mind fucking of all male deficiencies cannot be overstated.

It is still a hugely taboo subject among men. Even with today's liberal attitude toward sex and the over-the-counter availability of a variety of drugs that can help men with ED, the vast majority of us who suffer from it simply don't talk about it to other men— and certainly not among my Italian male friends. I couldn't even tell my own cousins that their homemade wine tasted like old socks dipped in paint stripper. Can you imagine how impossible it would be to admit to one another that your man bits didn't work? Instead, we men surreptitiously seek help and advice from doctors and andrologists, or we order pills online. I went for the doctor approach.

"Don't worry, Pellegrino. It's very common," chirped the doctor as she filled out my patient journal.

Yes, *she*. My regular *male* doctor had called in sick at the last minute. I know. I know. It shouldn't make a difference whether it's a male doctor or a female doctor. Only it does. Looking into the eyes of a woman, whatever her profession might be, or whatever her relationship to you is, and telling her that the *Homo sapiens* in front of her is not *Homo erectus* is definitely not something most men relish. Again, if you are one of those men who feels this does not apply to you, that you are so liberal-minded, gender-blind, and a general all-around hipster of the modern age, then congratulations—and again, fuck off!

Around the time I was experiencing my problems, I saw a TV interview with a celebrity who had just become an ambassador for erectile dysfunction. That person's name was Pelé. Yes, the very same Pelé that I had marveled at on my TV when I was a kid, way back in the seventies. The same Pelé my mother had named me Pelli after.

Pelé was sixty-two now and had just been signed up by pharmaceutical giant Pfizer to promote their new wonder drug, Viagra. It was also Pelé's job to create an open, honest discourse around erectile dysfunction, to try to dispel some of the taboo around ED.

During the interview, Pelé was asked if he had ever had erection problems, to which he replied incredulously: "Oh no, not me!" But it was the expression on his face that spoke volumes to me. The kind of look that communicated, "Do you know who I am? Do you not know that I was once the greatest footballer on the planet? Some would say the best footballer of all time. Do you not know that I was once a living, breathing icon of male accomplishment? Men like me don't suffer from erectile dysfunction!"

Some ambassador, I thought.

"But if I did suffer from erectile dysfunction," continued Pelé with a disproportionate amount of emphasis on the word *if*. "*If* I suffered from ED, I would speak to my doctor."

Which is what I am doing right now. Thanks for the advice, Pelé.

"Yes, it's very common," my female doctor continues encouragingly. "Anywhere between 15 and 25 percent of men suffer from it, and it's not just older men, either."

I wondered if she had sensed the air of self-reproach and self-contempt that had already enveloped my persona. Perhaps she was just saying this to make me feel better. That was nice of her. It was not working, though.

"But it's not a disease or an illness, Pellegrino. It's a symptom. Stress can be a big factor. Are you stressed at all, Pellegrino?"

Fuck, yes! Especially sitting here talking to you about ED. Not helping. Not helping at all!

"Do you have an erection when you wake up in the morning?"

"Uhm, yes, I think so . . ."

God! Am I really having this conversation? I think so? I know so!

I know she needs to ask me these questions. I just don't *want* her to ask me these questions. What I need now is a quick fix, a nudge in the right direction. This is taking way too long. And it's embarrassingly painful.

"Have you considered therapy? That might help you deal with the stress issues, because it's clear to me that your problem is psychological, not physical."

I can't hold it in any longer. I have to say something.

"Doctor, could you just prescribe me some Viagra?"

. . .

Viagra shares with Rizzolatti's macaque monkeys in Parma the fact that it was discovered completely by accident. Viagra's primary property is that it opens up the blood vessels, which is why it was originally designed to help people suffering from hypertension and angina. The hypothesis was that this new drug would alleviate the pressure of constricted arteries, allowing rejuvenating blood to flow more easily through the body.

Initial tests reported little effect for angina sufferers, but a remarkable propensity to induce erections. This story always makes me smile. Can you picture it? A lab full of men with high blood pressure, clasping their chests with one hand, trying to ease the pain of their angina, while at the same time clutching their very erect cocks with the other, their facial expressions a mix of incredulous dismay and blissful contentment.

As far as inducing a hearty hard-on is concerned, that magical, diamond-shaped, blue pill certainly did the trick. The only problem was, the first time I took one, my ancestry led me astray. I doubled the recommended dose—just in case.

You see, an expression you don't hear so often in Italian culture is "just enough." That expression belongs to the Nordic cultures, where frugality is an important value. You can see this when you look at the differences between eating habits in Norway and Italy. Growing up in the Riccardi household, we always served more food than was needed. Whenever we had family or friends over for dinner, my mother always made twice as much food as we actually needed, just in case someone was especially hungry or if an unexpected guest showed up.

"You never know," my mother would say. "It's better to have food and not need it than to need food and not have it."

The ultimate shame of any self-respecting southern Italian is not having enough food for your guests. This is even more shameful than not being able to muster up an erection at the drop of a hat, because at least nobody needs to know about the erection, whereas the whole table of guests would witness your lack of hospitality if you didn't have enough food for them.

Even today, whenever my sister makes her wonderful home-made pizzas in her hand-built pizza oven in her garden, she makes twice as many pizzas as she actually needs. Just in case.

"Just in case what?" I asked her the first time I saw her do this.

"Just in case, that's all," she replied, me none the wiser.

Fifteen guests to dinner? Let's make thirty pizzas, just in case. At her wedding, where they had almost two hundred guests, they served a total of fourteen courses. When I got married in Norway, the Norwegians served four. After the fourth, my father turned to me and asked what was for the main course!

And so it was with my first helping of Viagra. The doctor said to take one. So, you know, I took two. Just in case. The consequences were of megalodon proportions.

The ancient Chinese martial art of Iron Crotch Qi Gong has been around for over a thousand years. Even today, you can go and watch the toughest badass martial arts men compete in Iron Crotch championships, where they lift weights not with their arms but with their penis. The whole event is a bizarre spectacle where men wearing kilts to conceal their equipment stand on a couple of step stools, tie one end of a rope to their member, the other end to the weights, and then slowly lift the weight from the ground in a type of penile deadlift. I once saw a man deadlift over a hundred kilos, although the absolute world record for moving an object with a penis was set in 2017, when a kung fu master, Ye Hongwei, towed a helicopter along an airfield. A *helicopter*!

Let's just say that after my double dose of the magic blue diamond pills, I could have pulled a 747 jet out of its hangar. You could have secured a mooring line from the *Titanic* on to my cock and would have been safe in the knowledge that it would hold fast, even in a hurricane.

Iron Crotch Qi Gong is also said to improve one's sexual prowess by stimulating the flow of blood to the pelvic area and testicles. Kung fu master practitioners of Iron Crotch Qi Gong swear by it. There has even been a book written about it: *Healing Impotence the Traditional Chinese Way* by Guo Bao Wei.

Thankfully, here in the West, we opt for a more user-friendly, diamond-shaped, magic pill. The only problem is, of course, that once you opt for the blue pill, you are at the mercy of that blue pill's effects. Eternal life may well be the hope and dream of many a Catholic boy like myself, but an eternal .44 Magnum erection is simply not the same thing.

You see, the damn thing wouldn't go back in its holster, even after the lovemaking was over. For the next twenty-four hours, even the slightest microthought of anything remotely sexual or alluring caused it to salute and stand to attention like a meerkat keeping watch for its clan.

This proved to be both extremely inconvenient and highly embarrassing, especially if it happened in public places, like at the bus stop and at the supermarket checkout. I would be standing there with an erection that looked like the Leaning Tower of Pisa. As in, you think it's about to come down, but it never actually does.

And it ached. Oh, how it *ached*! A dull, throbbing, relentless aching, as if my cock was the key of a guitar head, pulling on a thick E-string that was attached to the bottom of my brain stem. Next time I took a blue pill, I was sure to take a more modest Nordic dosage.

Another problem with taking the blue pill is that it only solves a mechanical problem, not an emotional one. In *The Matrix*, Keanu Reeves's character, Neo, is offered the option of swallowing either a blue pill or a red pill. The red pill will take him down a deep rabbit hole of adventure and uncertainty, while swallowing the blue one will bring his dream and adventure to an end, allowing him to wake up in his bed again and believe whatever he wants to believe. The red pill represents knowledge, freedom, uncertainty, and, ultimately, the Truth—even if that truth is rather brutal. The blue pill, on the other hand, provides a false sense of security and a blissful ignorance of living an illusion. Neo took the red pill, and we ended up with act 2 of *The Matrix*.

I took the blue pill and entered a world of blissfully erected ignorance. It didn't matter how magnificent a manhood I displayed in the bedroom; the emotional side of our acts of intimacy was being slowly but irrevocably eradicated by countless rounds of testing, analysis, visits to doctors and fertility specialists, and on-demand babymaking sessions. My blue pill was fixing a mechanical problem in a completely mechanical production line.

The most ironic and paradoxical of it all was that the more iron my crotch became during performance, the greater the sense of emasculation I felt after I was done. I was a fraud. I was the Lance Armstrong of all *maestri fuckatori*. I could pout like a silverback, roar like a lion, while beneath the confident, cocky exterior, I was shriveling like an erectile dysfunctional cock in cold water.

Unsurprisingly, the little swimmers being ejected from my reproductive glands were as fake as their incompetent owner. Month after month, my wife would enter the bathroom, pregnancy test in hand, only to emerge again minutes later with that all-too-familiar look of despair. The months turned into years, and during those years, our bedroom saw progressively less action than the fertility clinic.

The story has a happy ending, though—a very happy ending. The IVF clinic helped us make two wonderful children, Christian and Emily. And let me just state for the record so there is absolutely no doubt whatsoever: I am eternally grateful to the doctors and specialists there for what they did for us. They helped enrich our life beyond words. And they were right all along: "Sooner or later, one way or another, the vast majority of women who want to get pregnant do get pregnant." Christian and Emily are the most precious beings, and life would simply not have been as magnificent without them.

All the same, on a masculine level, I was unable to smother the lie that continued to fester inside me. That somehow, I had cheated my way to fatherhood. That I was incomplete.

. . .

We settled down to the life of a bog-standard family with the two kids, a boy and a girl, in a quaint house in the Norwegian countryside with a lawn and a picket fence. The only thing missing from our apparently *Pleasantville* life was a Volvo parked in the driveway. But behind the idyllic façade of our home, with its welcoming porch and hanging baskets filled with brightly colored petunias and geraniums, my wife and I had entered a marital state that many parents of toddlers know too well: one that is filled with contrast and contradictions.

On one hand, we were eternally grateful for our newborns. People talk about the miracle of life, but most people don't fully appreciate what that means. I am pretty sure that IVF parents have a more acute understanding of what that "miracle" truly means. We actually got to see firsthand exactly how difficult making a life can be. We also saw how so many other couples took getting pregnant for granted, oblivious of the fact that as many as one in four couples have fertility challenges and unexplained infertility.

I don't blame those normal couples for it. It *should* feel normal to make children. Most couples manage it fine. However, statistics suggest that worldwide, there are over ninety million couples struggling with unexplained infertility. That's 180 million people! That's almost the entire population of Nigeria, the seventh most populated country in the world. Statistics like that help you appreciate life when it happens.

That's why we appreciated Christian and Emily so much, perhaps a tad more than your average parent. They were wanted, longed for, and desperately desired by their parents. I believe they have felt that gratitude as they've grown up. I can see it when I look into their eyes today. I am sure they can see in our faces a reassuring radiance of wonderment and gratitude that they are part of our lives.

But, on the other hand, the whole process of manufacturing a baby—and it did become a manufacturing process—steadily eroded and eradicated all that was sensual and erotic in our marriage. While the blue diamonds fixed me mechanically, they did nothing for me erotically. They say that diamonds are a girl's best friend, but these blue diamonds were definitely not a boy's best friend. They were my best *fiend*.

Add to the equation the normal mind-numbing zombie existence of being a parent to two children who still haven't put their nappy days behind them, and you have the perfect *anaphrodisiac*. This anaphrodisiac was so deep and ingrained in the soul and the loins that it felt like not even an Italian double dose of the blue diamonds could counteract it.

My wife and I tried to cling on to what we had in common—the fact that we had been through it all together—and tried to use it to prop up our relationship. We had faced adversity, and we had survived it. Most importantly, we had survived it together. Surely, that meant something. Statistics show that, without assisted fertilization, we would have had, at best, a 4 percent chance of conceiving naturally. We had defied the odds. And we had done it together. Surely, that must warrant staying together. Surely, we were meant for each other now. But the flame of our love and passion had dwindled to the flicker of an IKEA tea light. There was simply no escaping this fact. Our sailboats now seemed to be drifting in opposite directions.

Then the most unexpected and least imaginable thing happened. My wife got pregnant!

I'd been doing a lot of traveling with work, even more than normal. It was autumn, which is peak season in my line of work. Calendar days were merging into one big hectic blur, with no respite until the Christmas break. I couldn't remember if I was coming or going. What I do remember is that I was spending more nights in hotel beds than in my own bed. It was a Wednesday evening. I'd just walked in the door, in time for dinner with the family. My wife was preparing the food in the kitchen. She had her checked apron on. She was smiling.

"Hi, love," I sighed. "God, am I glad to be spending the night at home for a change. Guess who I saw on the plane today. You remember—"

"I'm pregnant."

Cue dumbfounded silence.

"Well, aren't you going to say something?" my wife asks me.

They say that your entire life flashes before your eyes the second before you die. Scientists refer to it as having an LRE—a life review experience—which they define as "an immediate moment of reliving significant past events." The hypothesis is that as we draw our final breath and blood stops flowing to the brain, the part of the brain that stops functioning last of all is the area associated with memory storage. The last thing we experience before the final flame of life is snuffed out is a neurological photo album of our most powerful memories. The longer the life, the bigger the photo album. But since the brain doesn't want to spend its final seconds browsing through tens of thousands of pages of photo album memories, it filters out the most vivid ones, those that are the most emotionally charged.

When my wife uttered those words—"I'm pregnant"—it's not like I had my entire life flash before my eyes. I wasn't about to die. After all, she was bringing me wonderful news. And it involved the *beginning* of life, not the ending of it. All the same, I did have an immediate moment of reliving significant past events—a mini-LRE. They were past events from the last nine years of becoming and being a father, the most emotionally charged of which I had collated into a neurological photo album. My album had memories that included the following:

- Blind, directionless sperm with huge learning disabilities
- A doctor's hand up my anal tract to untwist my epididymis
- White lady-slippers shuffling along a shiny linoleum corridor
- A masturbatorium
- Hairy Hungarian porn stars
- Blue diamonds
- An Iron Crotch Qi Gong erection that looked like the Leaning Tower of Pisa
- A submissive hyena with an erection
- A thermometer to measure basal body temperature
- A hissing wife with a high-pitched voice
- A huge question mark over a picture of a man
- Three petri dishes
- Three separate blastocysts, two of which are now called Christian and Emily.
- And a partridge in a pear tree

"Well, say something then!" my wife says again, a hint of urgency creeping into her voice, perhaps even trepidation at my dumbfounded and extended silence. Is that why they call it a pregnant pause?

The words that did finally drop out of my open-jawed mouth surprised even me. But when you hear them, I trust that you will understand why I said exactly these words, considering all the shit I'd been through for the past nine years.

"Who have you been shagging?"

"Nobody!" my wife answered, half amused, half insulted. "Really, nobody else!"

We hugged each other, this time in joy, not grief. We didn't need to say anything else. She totally understood why I'd said those words. She got it. She also got that this was a pivotal point in our lives. In *my* life. This moment will surely flash before my eyes in the last minutes of this life as one of the happiest.

Olivia Rosa Riccardi was born on July 7, 2011. Much to my relief, and perhaps even her mother's, Olivia was the spitting image of her father, laying to rest forever any suspicion or doubt as to whom my wife had been shagging.

More importantly, though, she was "made" without any assistance from test tubes, petri dishes, latex-gloved anal invasions, or plastic cups. For sure, Olivia's brother and sister were miracles of the laboratory, but Olivia was a miracle of nature, a miracle of God.

So, I ask you both now, God and Mother Nature, how and why can you allow our Olivia to wander toward that drawing at the bottom of the swimming pool? And don't give me that crap about free will. Please! Because, just as God had forsaken his Son, so too had Mother Nature forsaken her daughter as she descended quietly into the pool, deeper and deeper into that chlorine water on that hot, unforgiving summer's day.

CHAPTER 13

Pappa's Here

Olivia is sleeping on my lap. She is just fifteen days old. Newborn babies can take up to sixty breaths a minute when they are awake and as few as twenty when they sleep. When you consider that adults average between twelve and twenty, you begin to realize the sheer work rate of a pair of newborn lungs. Olivia's averaging around thirty right now.

When you have a newborn baby asleep on your lap, there's not much more you can do than watch them sleep and count their breaths. This is what has captivated my attention for the last half an hour or so. All of a sudden, and without warning, Olivia takes an extra deep, long breath in and holds it—one, two, three, four long seconds—before exhaling again through her nostrils and returning to her normal respiratory rhythm.

When you have a newborn baby asleep on your lap, you have little choice but to be in the moment—and maybe do some arithmetic in your head, like figuring out how many breaths Olivia has taken so far in her life. Let me see now: Newborns sleep for at least 16 hours a day, so let's say she averages 40 breaths per minute. . . . That's 2,400 per hour . . . which is . . . 58,000 per day, give or take a couple of hundred. . . . She's 15 days old, so . . . that's . . . 58 times 10, plus half of that, and don't forget to add the three zeros . . . 870,000! In just 15 days, her lungs have inhaled and exhaled 870,000 times. If she lives to be 80, she will take around 700 million breaths.

It's a dreary July day in Norway. The rain has been falling for a couple of hours now. It's not heavy rain, but somehow it has managed to drench everything in sight, including the rather conspicuous, brightly colored socks the kids have left strewn all over the lawn. They always take them off before they go on the trampoline; their bare feet get a better grip, apparently. The socks look so sad lying there on that soggy lawn, lifeless L-shapes forsaken in the July rain.

My roses and rhododendrons look happy, though, as do the Norwegian pine trees that blanket the hills. I have become well acquainted with those hills on my frequent bike rides. My favorite time of day to go biking is late afternoon, around five o'clock. That's when I head out toward an area of the forest called Krokskogen, which is just over the hillside, west of my house.

Krokskogen is perched high above Norway's fifth-largest lake, Tyrifjorden. Until today, nobody outside Norway—in fact, not many in Norway—had ever heard of this place. Tyrifjorden has three small islands in it: Frognøya, Storøya, and Utøya. One of these islands is about to become very, *very* famous.

There has been little time for bike rides since Olivia came into our world fifteen days earlier, though. And even if I'd had the time today, I'm sure I would have taken one look at the July rain and wimped out.

Instead, I will content myself with live coverage of the Tour de France on TV. The Tour is at stage nineteen of twenty-one, the classic Alpe d'Huez, where riders will haul their already fatigued bodies up to the finish line some 1,850 meters above sea level. It's a relatively short mountain stage of the tour—"brief and horrible" was the way one cycling correspondent described it—but one that never fails to excite and one that always sorts out the men from the minnows. Even with the volume turned down, the muted shouts and screams of encouragement from the fans that line the narrow ascent are palpable in my living room.

Olivia flinches again, momentarily. According to the pediatrician, this is a recalibration of her sensorimotor system—nothing to worry about. That's right: For now, Olivia Rosa Riccardi has nothing to worry about. She is safe. She is lying on her father's lap, a fifteen-day-old, four-kilo lump of inhaling, exhaling flesh and bone, her soft, fluffy head resting on my hands. She is so fragile and so utterly reliant on me to keep her safe from harm. I have rarely felt more needed by another human being. Also, I have seldom felt so physically larger than another human being. I am a giant in comparison to my Olivia, which, right now, is a good thing.

There is something particular—extraordinary—about a father soothing his daughter with his giant voice. Their mother sings to them. That works too. She has a lovely voice, her dulcet tones often filling our home as she goes about her day. My voice is no singing voice. My voice makes "Twinkle, Twinkle, Little Star" sound like it's being sung by a bear with a toothache.

What I can do well is hold a single note, a humming sound, a bit like the oscillating tone of a didgeridoo, a bit like the purring of a fat cat, or even the murmur of a vintage car engine. My kids love this sound. It works especially well first thing in the morning before I've had my first coffee; late at night is good too or when I have a sore throat. When I hold my children in my giant arms, I know they feel safe. There is something about the sound, combined with my comparative physical stature that provides my kids with a layer of protection from the outside world. Sometimes, I hold them so close to me that they can feel the beating of my heart through my chest cavity wall, so close that they can feel the deep baritones of my voice.

"Pappa's here," I murmur into the top of Olivia's head as I hold her close to me, one hand cupping her tiny behind, the other one cradling her fragile, sleepy head as it rests just beneath my left collar bone. The mellow, resonant booming of my voice seems to lull her even deeper into her slumber. "Pappa's here."

Outside, I hear a distant roll of thunder, rumbling as deep as my voice, if not deeper. A few minutes later, there is an unscheduled break in the coverage of the Tour de France. We go straight over to the news desk in Oslo: an explosion in the city center. That's only fifteen kilometers away from where I live. Could that have been the thunder I just heard?

The images on the TV are shocking and otherworldly, bizarrely out of place and out of context. It doesn't take long to draw the obvious conclusion. This is an act of terror. This can't be happening in Oslo, home of the Nobel Peace Prize, where Norwegians are so calm, so reasonable, so serene. This must be somewhere else. New York? Again? Surely not! Besides, the buildings on the TV aren't tall enough. London? Not enough people in the streets. The writing on the emergency vehicles tells me that the pictures are definitely being beamed from the Norwegian capital: *Ambulanse. Lege. Politi.* This *is* Norway. So many emergency vehicles, all lined up along the pavement, their personnel tending to the casualties.

I reach for the remote control to unmute the sound. But wait. Olivia will wake up if I do that. I leave the remote where it is.

A silent red no. 37 bus stands solitary in the street, halted in its tracks at a pedestrian crossing. The red bus sticks out among the dusty, debris-filled chaos, like the girl with the red jacket in *Schindler's List*. Its distinctive color is a poignant contrast to the mêlée of neon yellow emergency service vehicles. It is also the only object around that has all its windows intact. All around that empty bus, the ground is sprinkled with shattered glass and splintered shards, every window within a hundred-meter radius blown out of its frame by what we would learn later was a 950-kilo bomb packed into a Volkswagen Crafter van.

The same apocalyptic images fill the screen on every channel— at least, all the Norwegian channels. I want to turn the TV off, but I can't. I am transfixed, petrified, just like Peter. I lose track of time.

Eventually, the news images switch to another location, the screen split in two: On one side is a news reporter; the other is a row of tents in front of a hut. It must be an archive photo, because the sky in the photo is blue, not doomsday gray like today's. With the sound still turned down so as not to wake my daughter, I direct my eyes at the text for more information. All it says is *Astrid Randen: Reporter, Utøya*.

I gasp. Utøya. I know that place. It's in Tyrifjorden. That's where I would have been now, riding my bike, if I hadn't been tending to Olivia or if I hadn't wimped out because of the weather.

I reach for the remote control again. If Olivia wakes up now, so be it. I need to hear what's going on. Sure enough, Olivia stirs then wakes. I lower her back on to my lap. I have one eye on her, one eye on the screen. It doesn't take long for her to find my gaze and turn it into a two-eyed one. How can I deny her all my attention, even if a violation of humanity is unfolding just over the pine-tree forests to the west of us? I attempt a smile. It's not easy. But she doesn't deserve to see the fear in my face. Olivia smiles back at me, her mirror neurons too underdeveloped to sense the trepidation behind my smile.

"Pappa's here," I say again. "Pappa's here." But my voice has lost some of its conviction.

That thundering, rolling, distant rumble I'd heard earlier—it *was* the explosion. Just fifteen kilometers away! There was so much broken glass, the people dazed and just standing there on the streets of Armageddon. Police and various security personnel were trying to chaperone them away from the bomb site.

A feeble scream breaks the tragedy. But it's not coming from the television. It's Olivia. I pick her up again and hold her to my chest. She is warm. She is safe. But a sense of anxiety is welling up inside me.

Who would attack Norway in this way? And why? And in July too, the official summer holiday month in Norway, when all but the most essential businesses pull down their shutters for the month, when families vacate their suburban neighborhoods and head for their summer cabins or charter holidays. July is the month in Norway when nothing really happens. It's a month when you can't get ahold of anyone, whether it's to invite a neighbor over for a cup of coffee or to get someone to come and install a new water boiler in your house. Many of us immigrants simply refer to July in Norway as "Norwegian Ramadan." I used to joke to my fellow Norwegians that if anyone wanted to invade Norway, they should do it in July, when nobody is around to defend the country. I won't be making that joke again, that's for sure.

The reports coming from the now uninterrupted coverage are sketchy at best. They are chaotic, often conflicting and unconfirmed, which only accentuates the sense of horror and dread. What there is *no* question about is that there are many casualties; we just don't know how many.

As I sit glued to my TV set with my newborn child resting against my now tense body, I am fed horrific images from the island that suggest the very worst. Leisure boats of all shapes and sizes, manned by local residents and holidaymakers, are ferrying survivors over the cold, choppy water toward the stretchers of ambulance personnel waiting for them on the muddy banks of Tyrifjorden. Teenagers wrapped in blankets collapse into the arms of anyone who will catch them, their faces stricken with agony and disbelief. They have seen atrocities that nobody should have to see.

I wrap my giant arms around Olivia. "It's okay, Olivia. Pappa's here. Pappa's here." But the conviction is gone from my words. All that remains is hope, and a prayer.

. . .

It isn't until the next morning that the full extent of the carnage is confirmed: Sixty-nine dead on the island. Eight in Oslo. Countless maimed or injured. A nation in complete shock. More disturbing images emerge in the aftermath. There are bodies everywhere, their lives snuffed out like tea lights. Some are found in fetal positions, half-buried by the thick forest undergrowth. Others are slumped over grassy knolls and moss-covered rocks, their brightly colored red, blue, and orange rain jackets a futile camouflage against the lush green backdrop. I remember seeing those images and being oddly reminded of my children's socks strewn across the sodden lawn outside.

As the days pass and we try to process the enormity of this calamity, we begin to piece together the time line of events. Hundreds of youngsters, mostly teenagers, all of them members of the Youth Labour Party, had gathered on the island of Utøya for what should have been another idyllic annual conference and summer camp, a place where the country's future Labour Party politicians could meet and discuss important issues, as well as hear speeches from past and present party activists, politicians, even prime ministers. Utøya was like a breeding ground for the future of the Labour Party, for Norway, they hoped. Utøya was where the seeds of the party's future harvest were to be sown.

The Norwegian prime minister had been to many Utøya gatherings himself as a young Labour Party member, and he lost many personal friends in the attack. His sorrow was real, his tears authentic as he tried to offer words of comfort. The king received a standing ovation for his live address to the country a month later, a speech where he openly shed tears—as their king but mostly as a parent and a grandfather. He told us that he could only imagine the torment and pain the parents of the victims must be feeling. He was right. We could only imagine. And every time I imagined losing one of my three children on that island, alone, desperate, and forsaken, my mirror neurons fired into action, and my imagination suddenly became the dull pain of reality.

As the weeks passed, one disturbing story more than any other began to fall into place, one important piece of the jigsaw puzzle that led to that fateful day's final outcome. It was a detail that the foreign media in particular homed in on right away: The unspoken consensus, not only in Norway but around the world, was that the Norwegian Emergency Response Unit—a.k.a. *Beredskapstroppen*, call sign *Delta*—had failed to respond swiftly and effectively enough. They had shown themselves to be a group of flagrantly incompetent men. Indeed, the whole chain of events from the time the bomb went off at 15:25 to when Anders Behring Breivik was finally in police custody at 18:34 reads like a catalog of errors, flaws, and resource mismanagement blunders.

It started from the moment a member of the public called in with a detailed description of the killer, including the van he had fled the Oslo bombing scene in, a gray Fiat Doblò, registration number VH 24605. That reliable tip-off was then written down on a yellow Post-it Note and placed on the desk of a superior at the command center. That superior happened to be on the phone and did not see the note until more than two hours later, by which time the killer had already arrived on the island and set about slaying his victims.

A Post-it Note! Are you fucking kidding me? Your country is under attack and you place your best lead to intercepting the perpetrator on a Post-it Note on someone else's desk? Post-it Notes are for reminding yourself to buy milk, or to-do lists, not for passing on the most important piece of information in a national manhunt.

Instead of setting up roadblocks around Oslo or announcing the plate number on the national radio to alert the general public, the authorities did nothing. The killer was allowed to carry out part two of his plan. He got into a rental van, which he had parked close by and which held a heavy plastic box full of weaponry, and he drove from Oslo city center to the Utøya ferry stop. The distance from the center of Oslo to the ferry is forty kilometers, a drive that under normal driving conditions takes around forty-five minutes. On this dreary, rainy July day, it would take him eighty-five min-utes—nearly twice as long as usual. For eighty-five minutes, he sat in his Fiat Doblò, registration number VH 24605, navigating heavy traffic while he listened to news reports on the radio about what he had just done. For eighty-five minutes, the police, the special forces, and thousands of Norwegian citizens failed to do anything about it. And all that time, a forgotten Post-it Note's corners were already starting to curl upward.

The tragic sequence of events continued with poor communication channels and failure at every level. Stories emerged of local police officers who ignored direct orders to drop what they were doing and provide immediate assistance at the scene. One of these police officers was in the middle of transporting a prisoner from one jail to another. Another was dealing with a psychiatric patient at a nearby institution. Neither task was essential or life threatening. Neither task needed to be dealt with there and then. But both those officers decided to ignore the order and instead finish up their own business before attending to a national crisis. I can only imagine what they were thinking: *Well, it's four o'clock, time to go home soon and tuck into my regular Friday night Mexican food. It would be a shame not to finish off what I started. And, besides, it's Norwegian Ramadan.*

All this time, Breivik was allowed to continue his murdering of defenseless, innocent children. At 18:01—after exactly forty minutes of cold-blooded slaughter—the assassin picked up a mobile phone from the ground, one of the many that had fallen alongside their lifeless owners, and called the police to inform them that he had completed his mission and would like to hand himself in. For whatever reason, the person who answered the call was hesitant and indecisive, fumbling for an appropriate way to respond to the caller. The result of this indecision was that the killer became more aggravated and frustrated, so he hung up and continued with his killing for another twenty-five minutes.

At 18:26, Breivik called again from another orphaned mobile phone. He was spoiled for choice by now. Cellular devices were scattered all around him, ringing, vibrating, their screens lighting up like fireflies in the damp light of dusk as desperate parents tried to get through to their sons and daughters. Again, he identified himself, and again, he informed the police that his mission was complete and that they could come and arrest him. And again, an equally indecisive, perhaps shell-shocked, telephone operator failed to deal effectively with the call. So, for one last time, Anders Behring Breivik was allowed to stroll around the island for another eight minutes, picking off his final victims before being finally apprehended at 18:34.

The very last victims he shot were five despairing souls who were cowering for safety behind the island's pump house on the southern tip of the island. This is the image that haunts me the most: those five souls facing their inevitable fate. How many breaths per minute did *they* take in those final moments? In my nightmares, it is many more than the thirty breaths per minute Olivia draws as she sleeps on my lap. What I know for sure is that none of those final five victims had come anywhere close to their lifetime quota of seven hundred million as they fell to the ground, slumped over the soaked shoreline rocks and grassy knolls, five lifeless L-shapes forsaken in the July rain.

We failed them. And when I say "we," I mean men. After all, it would have probably been men who apprehended the killer as he sat in traffic on the way to the ferry and then sat through the ferry ride. It was men's job to protect those children as their powerless, paralyzed parents watched on in horror. It was men who failed to protect those who were not able to protect themselves.

One enduring image that I haven't been able to erase from my memory is of a small red dinghy, overladen with ten Emergency Response Unit members, all men and all armed to the hilt and squished up against each other, put-putting across the fjord like some inflatable tuk-tuk, its engine choking on the water that was pouring in over the side and flooding its fuel lines. It would take the vigilant response of a local resident to come to the rescue in his own personal leisure boat, which the ERU were able to transfer to and head for the island. If ever there was an image that epitomizes incompetence, impotence, and inadequacy, then the image of that red dinghy is it.

What good are we men if we fail to accomplish the one task that we are supposed to be better equipped for than women? The one competitive edge we have over women, that Mother Nature herself bestowed on us—our physical size and strength.

It took eight months for the police to apologize. And when the apology did come, it was only after intense public pressure, and it came in the form of an internal police investigation, which pinpointed fifty-four "Learning Points." Learning points? Not mistakes. Not errors. Not incompetence. Not fuck-ups. Learning points. God, I hate euphemisms! And it was described as a system failure. Not human failure. Not *men* failure. System failure.

The "apology" felt hollow and incomplete. Lots of ifs and buts, should-haves and could-haves, but never an actual, fullhearted, unequivocal, unconditional apology. Not that an apology would have turned back time, but it could have served as a soothing balm for the gaping wounds those parents were trying to heal.

An apology is not only a healing balm. It also acts as a form of closure, a foundation on which to rebuild. Whether it is for a minor wrongdoing or misdemeanor, or for a serious offense or betrayal, a genuine, remorseful apology prepares the path for reconnection and reconciliation. An apology makes way for the forgiveness of others and, more importantly, of oneself.

What those kids on the island needed was a group of determined alpha males to come and use their physical presence and force to intervene in a heinous, abhorrent act. Those children needed those alpha males to act with resolve, precision, and a sense of urgency. Those babies—and they were all babies to their parents—needed those men in the red dinghy to wrap their giant arms around them and comfort them, soothe them, to whisper into their ears with their deep, rumbling baritone voices: "It's okay. I'm here. Pappa's here."

CHAPTER 14

Everything I Do, I Do It for You— Even the Nasty Stuff

I am twenty times heavier than Olivia was when I held her on my lap, but as I looked at how tiny she was in proportion to my limbs, it felt like I was twenty-five *hundred* times her size.

A psychologist friend of mine once explained that this is why we adults don't ever need to raise our voice to a child. "Your sheer size as an adult, especially as a man, is already more than enough to intimidate a child. And that's before you even open your mouth to speak," he told me.

From the perspective of a child, our giant-like proportions make us scary enough as it is, without having to shout at them. That's why raising your voice to a child defeats its purpose. It's complete overkill.

I was in town one day with Olivia, running some errands. With all the time I spent away from home with my work, I thought it would be a good idea to kill two birds with one stone and steal some time with her. Our itinerary included Starbucks, where Olivia would always ask for a Chocolate Crème Chip Frappuccino and a chocolate chip cookie. She certainly loves her chocolate. A few more years of this habit, I said to myself, and she will start to smell like my father when he came home from his night shift. We were waiting at a pedestrian crossing. Suddenly, Olivia decided to step out into the road.

"Oh, my God! Stop!" I screamed, yanking her arm half out of its socket as I wrenched her back to the safety of the pavement. "What the fuck were you trying to do? Are you stupid? You'll get yourself killed!"

It was my fault, of course. I should have been holding her hand tightly and reminding her how important it was to wait for the red man to turn to green. Instead, I was texting.

The obscenities that gushed out of my mouth terrified Olivia much more than the hypothetical collision with any oncoming car. Of course, I hadn't *meant* to scare her. There was absolutely no correlation between the blowtorch of words that came out of my mouth and the actual sentiments behind them. What looked and sounded on the outside like anger and contempt for my daughter was actually a deep sense of fear and shame. I was afraid of what could have happened and ashamed at the realization that such calamity would have been entirely my own fault. Had I been able to freeze-frame that moment in time and had I been able to rewrite the script with a calm and fully functional prefrontal cortex, my words would have been something like this: "Oh my

God, Olivia, you're about to cross the road and risk being run over. The reason you're about to do this is that I allowed myself to be distracted by my mobile device when I should really have been looking after you; after all, you're a child. You, Christian, and Emily are the most precious things in the world to me. If anything were to happen to you and—God forbid—if I were to lose you, I would never be able to live with myself."

So why not just say that, then? What is it in the workings of the human mind that preclude us from saying what is actually on our minds and in our hearts? One of the most important things I've learned over the years about people is that, behind every behavior, there is usually some kind of positive intent—even behavior that looks and sounds as vulgar and unreasonable as I'd displayed with Olivia. All too often, humans behave in ways that glow with positive intentions yet are tarnished by negative manifestations.

Our initial response to a situation is like that of any other animal; it is mostly determined by lightning-fast, instinctual reflex. In the heat of the moment, especially a moment of perceived emergency, we don't have as much control over our actions as we think. We don't have time for that, not if you want to stay alive at least. The normally docile and extremely shy elk that attacks a trekker during calving season does so to protect her offspring. The shark that attacks a surfer is not so much vicious and cold-blooded as she is curious or hungry or both.

What does distinguish humans from animals, though, is that humans will often regret their well-intentioned transgressions. I know I have—many times. It's what makes us human. The elk will just stampede you and walk away, its protected calf in tow, without so much as an ounce of remorse. And it's not as if the shark will realize she's just ripped off your leg, apologize, and offer to call you an ambulance. Animals operate according to pure instinct and evolutionary programming. Humans act like any other animal, but then we reflect later. I scream at Olivia first and keep her alive, but then I feel bad about scaring her half to death and apologize later.

Behaviors that lead to some kind of reward, payoff, or positive outcome will get repeated. Repeated behaviors become habits. Habits that are adopted by a critical mass become a collective norm, or a culture. And if a collective norm crosses over from one generation to the next, it becomes a custom. Get that custom to last for *thousands* of generations, and it becomes part of our genetic makeup, our auto-response system. This is why we instinctively recoil at the sight of a rattlesnake and become all gooey-eyed when we see an infant bear cub crying out for its mother.

But environment can change all of that. Put the snake behind two inches of glass at the zoo, and we might well move *closer* to the snake to get a better look. And our gooey eyes would quickly lose all their gooiness if we suddenly realized that we were standing a few feet away from that bear cub's mother. Environment also has the final say over our genetic programming, the final edit, or, as Dr. Judith Stern of the University of California neatly put it, "Genetics may load the gun, but environment pulls the trigger."[1]

---

1 Hillary Rodham Clinton, "Now Can We Talk about Health Care?" *New York Times Magazine,* April 18, 2004, https://www.nytimes.com/2004/04/18/magazine/now-can-we-talk-about-health-care.html.

Environment was the reason my grandparents had so many children. It was considered the best way to beat the infant mortality rate statistics of postwar, poverty-stricken Italy, with its poor hygiene and sanitation, malnutrition, and a nonexistent welfare system. The chances of your children making it to fully fledged adulthood were a lot worse than they are now. So, what type of behavior was best suited to compensate for this adverse environment? Easy. Just procreate a couple of extra children. You know, just in case.

In my father's family, for example, there were seven brothers and sisters. Five made it to adulthood while two died before the age of ten. On my mother's side, they went for six kids. Against all the odds, all six made it to adulthood, but only three of them survived long enough to draw their pension, while the other three suffered from poor health for most of their adult lives.

And can you imagine what it was like if we go even further back in time to when the first ever Riccardis roamed the savannah? It doesn't take too much of a stretch of the imagination to understand how hostile a world *they* lived in, a world in which death was as likely to come from an infected cut on your little finger as it was from a ferocious predator. With such odds stacked so highly against them, we can begin to appreciate just how much procreating they really had to do just to keep the population balance sheet in the black.

Meanwhile, nature and biology determined that whenever a woman became pregnant, she would be unable to procreate for the next nine months. She could still have sex, but it would not propagate the human race. Besides, her pregnancy hormones would be kicking in and slowly but surely turning down her libido levels.

That was not the case for men, whose raging loins would be on the lookout for ways to propagate and pass on their genes. Darwinism demanded they do so. To refrain from doing so would be to put the survival of the species at risk. For a man to have fifty girlfriends makes complete evolutionary sense. But for a woman to have fifty boyfriends has no evolutionary purpose. Not only that, but nine months is a long time to wait for a horny *Homo erectus*. A multitude of awful episodes could happen to that man during that nine-month period of time, which would, in effect, rob him of his chance to create more valuable offspring. This meant that men had a moral obligation to fuck as many women as humanly possible. So they did. You know, just in case.

And so it came to be that one of the most important codes of man's genetic programming was scripted into his psyche. And God saw what he had made, and—behold!—it was very good. Even God acts first and reflects later, it would seem. Oh, and by the way, *that's* how we know that God is a man and not a woman. A woman would *never* have created such a genetic script. And she would never have invented snoring, either.

· · ·

Why on earth do people snore? Well, there too we find a "positive" evolutionary explanation. Evolutionary psychologists hypothesize that snoring developed as a way to protect ourselves from predators while we lay asleep in our caves and our trees.

Think about it. *Homo erectus* is lying there fast asleep, the last flames of his campfire about to die out. He is vulnerable. He is alone. Along comes an angel and whispers into his ear: "Hey, you! Sleepyhead! Something terrible is about to happen. There's a leopard sneaking up on you. Wake up!"

Homo erectus stirs in his sleep and mumbles something about leaving him alone. He's tired. He's had a hard day chasing antelopes. They were too fast for him. All he got to eat that day was some measly berries and a handful of mushrooms, and he is not even sure they were safe to eat.

The angel tries again. "Hey! Something *really* terrible is about to happen if you don't wake up. That leopard looks really hungry. He didn't catch any antelope either."

Homo erectus doesn't respond, his REM eyelids flickering away as he enters the deepest stage of sleep. He thinks the angel is just part of some trippy dream he's having, possibly brought on by those dodgy mushrooms.

The angel turns to more drastic measures. She pinches his nostrils with her fingers and stops him breathing. To compensate for the sudden loss of air, *Homo erectus* opens his mouth to breathe, his tongue drops into the back of his mouth, and out comes that all-too-familiar rasping sound that has plagued sleeping partners ever since.

It's a nasty sound. Raucous. Grating. But it's a sound that frightens the leopard away.

The angel sees an opportunity here and reports back to God that there is no need to send out any more angels to warn sleeping

Homo erectus. He can look after himself now. He has developed the ability to snore. And God saw what he had made, and—behold! It was very good.

Over time, the snoring became louder, because *Homo erectus* realized pretty quickly that the louder he snored, the scarier he would be to any potentially dangerous animal lurking around outside. Even better would be if his woman snored too. Unfortunately, this was more the exception rather than the rule. If *Homo erectus* happened to live and sleep in a cave, he was practically invincible, since that cave would act as an amplifier and loudspeaker for his snoring, making him sound even more powerful and capable of looking after himself. Soon, the biggest snorers of the tribe gained the greatest status among their peers. They were also the people who slept safest at night. People would actually *want* to sleep near the man with the loudest snore and the biggest cave. Perhaps this is why, even today, the rich and powerful build themselves such big "caves" in places like Beverly Hills in Los Angeles, Hampstead in London, and Holmenkollen in Oslo.

Nowadays, the snore is a redundant attribute. Nobody feels safe sleeping next to a loud snorer anymore. My wife certainly doesn't. She once described my snoring as sounding like an orc, one of those ugly creatures from *The Lord of the Rings*, the ones who serve the evil Sauron. An orc with a dust bunny stuck down its throat, she said.

I thought this was rather harsh, at least until, one night, my wife recorded my snoring with her phone. What I heard when I played back the recording truly shocked me. I really did sound like an orc with a dust bunny stuck down its throat. And the snoring didn't seem to stop, either. It was persistent, incessant, unrelenting.

"At least I'm keeping you safe from potential predators!" I said in a feeble attempt to lighten the mood. But my wife didn't get the reference or the joke, and soon after, we'd changed our one double duvet to two single duvets. "Oh, it was because double duvet covers are so limited in choice nowadays," she claimed, "so we might as well buy single duvets, where the selection of covers is much larger." After that, it became more and more difficult to feel her skin whenever I stretched out my arm in the bed, my exploratory fingers being met instead by a tightly wound-up cocoon of feather and down.

It didn't take long before she started leaving our bed in the middle of the night to go and sleep in the spare room. There is nothing quite as sad and lonely as waking up in the morning, reaching out to touch your partner, and finding instead that she has left you. *What happened to all that in sickness and in health shit?* I asked myself. In good times and bad times? My mother complained about my father's snoring too, but they always woke up in the same bed.

Logically, it made complete sense to me that my wife would seek nocturnal solace in another room. Sleep deprivation is certainly not to be taken lightly. Emotionally, though, I was struggling to accept it, and emotions drive our actions much more than logic. So I set about curing my snoring. Because that's what men like to do—you know, fix things.

Operation Silent Sleeper, Phase 1: The Anti-snoring Gumshield

I set up an appointment with a sleep specialist, who informed me that there were a number of ways to deal with snoring. One of them was to have a special gumshield made, one that would force my lower jaw out beyond my upper jaw, opening my throat up so that the fatty tissue of my throat, like the uvula—that "boxing bag" piece of gristle that hangs down at the back of the mouth—couldn't vibrate with the tongue or the tonsils.

So off to the dentist I went. The dentist fixed me up with the gumshield. It worked quite well too, but I had to stop after a few weeks, for two main reasons.

The first reason was vanity. I would like to be able to say that my nocturnal protruding jaw made me look like Marlon Brando in *The Godfather*. Even Jay Leno would have worked for me. Sadly, though, I looked more like Bubba from *Forrest Gump*.

The second reason was pain. A night of lockjaw may have stopped the snoring, but every morning I would wake up with the mother of all headaches—throbbing pain in my temples, a dull ache in my jaw, like I'd done ten rounds with Mike Tyson. After a night of that gumshield, I even talked like Mike Tyson. Operation aborted.

Operation Silent Sleeper, Phase 2: New Front Teeth

While I was at the dentist having my gumshield made, he discovered that I had managed to grind down my front teeth to half their original size. The dentist asked me if I was under stress or suffered from anxiety, since anxiety, he explained to me, often manifests itself subconsciously during sleep. This would then cause prolonged periods of teeth gnashing.

"Perhaps," I replied. "I suppose things have been a little tough recently, what with . . ."

But before I could recount my sob stories of alienation and disillusionment from my life and my wife, he'd already stuffed the saliva ejector in my mouth and had started sizing up my new teeth.

"Mmm, oh dear, yes, I see," he murmured reassuringly. "Your teeth have been ground down to the gums in some places, which has also forced other teeth in your mouth to point different directions." So we agreed to rebuild my front teeth too, and when I say "we," I actually mean *he* agreed.

What my dentist didn't tell me was that, at the end of my teeth-building procedure, my tongue would have to relearn where my alveolar ridge was. The alveolar ridge is the part of the roof of the mouth where the upper teeth and the hard palate meet. The alveolar ridge is also the part of your mouth that the tongue needs to make precise contact with in order to produce so-called alveolar consonants. These are the *t*, *d*, *s*, and *z* sounds. It's a very small area, only a matter of a millimeter or two, but if the tongue doesn't hit exactly the right spot on the alveolar ridge, then you end up lisping. So, instead of *t*, *d*, *s*, and *z* coming out of your mouth, you end up with *th*, *th*, *th*, and *th*.

As a public speaker, this was obviously going to be a problem for me, especially since what I talk about most of the time is communication. So, for the next month, I would step up on to the stage and declare to the audience: "Hello everyone, my name ith Pellegrino Riccarthi, and I am a communicathons exthperth."

As for my snoring—or should I say, my *sthnoring*—well, that remained unchanged.

Operation Silent Sleeper, Phase 3: Tonsillectomy

The gumshield had failed. My alveolar consonants were all over the place. But there was one more option, another way to reduce the unwanted fleshy friction in my throat: a tonsillectomy. By removing my tonsils, the surgeon assured me, there would be less tissue to vibrate against the soft palate, and so the snoring would be reduced.

Sounded logical to me. Let's give it a shot, I declared. Third time lucky, I cried, excited and optimistic that I had finally found the answer. The surgeon seemed optimistic and confident.

The surgeon was wrong.

It didn't work at all. And that wasn't all. If I thought that the gumshield had been painful or that lisping on stage in front of large audiences was distressing, both of those paled in comparison to the misery that I was about to experience with the removal of my tonsils. They say that the later in life you have your tonsils removed, the more it hurts. I had no idea how true that statement would prove to be.

Once the anesthetic wore off, all I had to help with the pain were the painkillers the hospital gave me, which came in the form of—yes, you guessed it—suppositories! Of course. What else would they be? Memories of seventies sunburn started flooding back to me and triggering my gag-reflex sphincter. Only this time, I didn't have an obliging, selfless mother to turn to. The only mother around was the mother of my children, and I couldn't really ask her to help me out, however much pain I was in or how completely out of my mind I was on opioids.

Can you imagine having *that* conversation? "Darling, I know I've kept you up night after night with my orc-like snoring, but would you mind terribly sticking a pill up my arse four times a day for the next seven days? I promise I won't look at you, and I promise not to let my sphincter spit it back out at you like I did with my mother."

Self-administering the suppositories it was, then—four pills a day for seven days. It was not exactly the ten thousand hours of "purposeful practice" that Malcolm Gladwell wrote about in his *New York Times* best seller *Outliers*, but it was enough to be able to call myself a bit of an expert in sphincter penetration by the end of it. Besides, I would be snore-free soon, right?

Wrong. I still snored like an orc with a dust bunny down its throat. But at least I'd tried.

And this is the point that I want to make. I tried. I tried for *her*. Not for myself, for *her*. Snoring never bothered me. I'm fine with it. The only reason I would ever consider inflicting on myself a ridiculous gumshield, or month of lisping, or an agonizing tonsillectomy, along with twenty-eight rounds of sphincter-stuffing pill taking was to make my woman happy! That's what it's all about for me: Happy wife, happy life.

I suspect that's what it's all about for lots of other men too. If I can make my woman happy by loving her, honoring her, protecting her, even serving her, it makes me feel good; it makes me feel complete.

I know how that last sentence reads. I know that I sound like one of King Arthur's Knights of the Round Table. I know that what I am saying now is painfully anachronistic and even politically incorrect. I know that my words sound condescending and patronizing. None of that, though, is my intention. It's not who I really am. Remember that, behind every behavior is usually some kind of positive intent or explanation. Behind the external manifestation of that condescending, patronizing male chauvinist you see lies nothing but a man with positive intentions, trying the best he can to make his woman happy. Why else would I go to the trouble of having my jaw practically rammed out of its socket or the flesh in the back of my throat cauterized by some crazy surgeon? I did that for *her*. It's one of the ways I try to show my love for her.

And all I ask for in return is one, simple favor. It's not even a favor, more a gesture—a token, if you like. All I ask in return is to be admired. Not liked, not appreciated, not idolized. *Admired*.

CHAPTER 15

Being in Love

I want to be admired like Rosa admires Luigi when he builds a shrine in the garden, or when he writes her name in white stones in his mosaic. Sadly, that hardly ever happens, and when it *does* happen, it's usually in winter, when the snow lies deep on the ground.

Every winter, here in Norway, we get pummeled by snow. It is not unusual to get a couple of meters of snow, which means I spend countless hours in the mornings, afternoons, and evenings clearing snow away from the entrance to our house and from the driveway that leads down to our subterranean garage. Armed with my snow shovel, I step into my snow boots, pull on a pair of heavy-duty work gloves, venture out into the winter wonderland outside my door, and start the task of clearing snow.

Nobody really likes clearing snow, not even the Norwegians. It's like doing the laundry or cleaning the toilet bowl. It's a shit job, but someone has to do it. To be honest, I would rather clean the toilet than clear the snow. At least I don't have to put on thermal underwear, goggles, and a woolly hat when I clean the toilet. As for me, I really, *really* hate clearing snow. But I do it *even though* I hate it.

I could hire someone else to do it for me. I could, but I don't. I do this job for her, for my woman. I *want* her to see me doing it. I want her to see me strutting around, flexing my muscles and displacing shitloads of snow, sinking my shovel down into the white powder, hoisting it up into the air and casting it over my shoulder into the void and out of the way. With every arching swoop and swoosh of that snow shovel, I am her snow-clearing peacock, my powder-pummeling prowess as ostentatious and histrionic as a peacock's shimmering plume.

I don't *need* to clear the snow, either. I have a four-wheel-drive, seven-seater monster of an SUV that can practically drive itself up a wall of snow. Without my dedicated snow clearing, though, my wife would struggle to make it up the ramp from our garage to the road in her car. She could, of course, pay for a snow-clearing service or buy a four-wheel-drive vehicle, but then she wouldn't be able to drive around in her cool little electric car, which I know she is very fond of. Also, what would our politically correct, eco-friendly Norwegian neighbors say if we had *two* four-wheel-drive combustion engine vehicles? It's bad enough with one.

No, I clear the snow because I want to show my Norwegian wife that I can measure up to any Nordic man when it comes to keeping one's house and garden in order, whatever the time of year. Nordic men know how to clear snow. So do Nordic women, by the way, although whenever I survey my neighborhood, it seems to be that the vast majority of those who clear the snow are men. It would seem that snow clearing is the one area of life women are only too happy to let the men "dominate."

And so it *should* be. Women already take on many more domestic responsibilities than men, even in the ultra-modern Nordic countries. Recent statistics tell us that it is still women who do most of the cleaning, spend most time with the children, and prepare the most food for the family. This is unfair to women, so it seems only right that we men assume responsibility for the snow.

Clearing my own snow, then, is a bit like my father growing his own plum tomatoes for his pasta sauce. He could easily buy them in the supermarket. They even say "Produced in San Marzano" on them. But they never taste quite as good as the ones he grows himself.

It's the same psychology that underpins a purchase at IKEA. The fact that you build an IKEA wardrobe or bookshelf yourself—even if that building process drives you half insane—means you attribute more value to the finished product than if you had bought it premade. Numerous psychological studies have verified this very phenomenon. It even has a name: *the IKEA effect*. When Luigi built his own house, he had a ten-year overdose of the IKEA effect. By clearing my own snow, I attribute more value to the final product: a snow-free, ice-free driveway.

In England people manicure their lawns, their hedges, and their gardens. In Norway, we manicure our driveways and entrances during the winter so that occupants and visitors to the homestead are provided with a safe and aesthetically pleasing passage up to the front door.

The amount of snow I clear each time varies from a few centimeters of fluffy white powder (a good day) to over a meter of heavy, wet snow (a bad day). The total area I have to clear around my house is about 160 square meters. Now, if the snow outside my door in the morning is a meter deep, and if it's wet snow as well, then I can look forward to shifting about 100,000 tons of the white stuff. In the super-snowy winter of 2018, when I counted fourteen major snow-clearing sessions, I shifted over a million and half tons of snow—by hand! This is another important factor to point out. I'm a purist: I clear my snow by hand. More and more men of middle-class suburbia in Norway have invested in a motorized snowblower or motorized mini snowplow. I, on the other hand, insist on doing it by hand.

During winter, walking from our garage up to our main entrance is like trekking through a World War I trench that has been doused in icing sugar. Every time it snows, I am out there making sure the pathway to our front door remains accessible and manicured, all winter long.

This is something that doesn't go unnoticed by many Norwegians in my neighborhood, who are quick to compliment me on my snow-clearing capabilities. At least, the *women* neighbors compliment me. The men neighbors *tell* me they are impressed, but behind their words of praise, I can't help noticing an air of resentment. My zealously manicured snow paths set a new standard for the neighborhood, a standard their wives back home are fully expecting their own men to emulate. Not only that, but the person setting that standard is not even a fellow Norseman.

He's a foreigner! From Italy! It's as bad as if a Norwegian living in Italy made better pizzas than his Italian neighbors.

But I don't care about all that. I couldn't care less if the men clear snow better than me or not. All I care about is *her*. All I care about is the moment when my wife drives up that steep ramp from the garage to the main road, when she looks at my face, bathed in sweat, my arm and back muscles oozing lactic acid, and she throws me that smile of gratitude and admiration. That's it.

It is but a fleeting moment, but beautiful nonetheless, a moment where no words are exchanged, a moment where I offer her my service and she graciously accepts. For just a second, I know that she admires me. She loves me. More importantly, for that one subliminal second, I know that we are in love again. Then she's gone. *It's* gone. Not the love, but the being in love. And there is a huge difference between *loving* someone and *being in love* with them.

Being in love with someone is a chemical state of mind and body, where one's dopamine, endorphin, and oxytocin levels have all spiked. It is a feeling of euphoria, a rush, a drug you simply can't get enough of. It is an addiction. Indeed, being in love exhibits all the hallmarks of drug addiction: the craving, the intoxication, the obsession of it all—not to mention the yearning and separation anxiety when your lover is not with you. In essence, being in love is a chemically induced form of madness, and it is a terrible foundation on which to build any kind of long-lasting relationship, which helps explain much of modern-day divorce rates.

And yet we want it, we seek it, we crave it. I know I do.

For the vast majority of people, this neurobiological state of being in love lasts for about two years—sometimes more, usually less. After that, after all the highs of the hormonal rush of your love trip ebb away, if you're lucky, you'll enter the *loving* stage. This is when levels of the more euphoric hormones dopamine and endorphin return to normal, leaving behind a residue of oxytocin, which is a more resilient and less fleeting hormone.

Some people believe that being in love lasts forever. It doesn't. It never does. No emotion is built to last forever, not even the ones that make you feel good. Emotions are, by definition, transitory, ephemeral, and fugitive. Love comes and goes. When it does come, you'll know. Just like when it goes, you'll know that too. You'll know when love is inside you. You'll know because you'll get that micromoment of warmth and connection with another living, breathing being.

When I stand over Olivia as she lies asleep in her bed, just watching her breathe—just watching her be alive—I feel it. When I imagine her edging her body into the cooling waters of that pool in Puglia, and I take her hand in mine and gently pull her out before she goes in too deep, I feel it. Every time I think of that, I can feel my heart is ready to burst.

And that's when I know that love hurts too. Love is pain. Love is the dull convulsive aching of regret. The love for a child, one's own child, is surpassed by no other love. It is the purest form of love a man can know.

Even Nazis loved their children. When Joseph and Magda Goebbels decided to poison their five daughters and their son, they did so out of love. From the outside looking in, their actions seem nothing like love. A parent who loves their child does not poison her! And yet, in a final letter that Magda Goebbels wrote before she executed her plans, she says that her children are "too precious for the life that will come."[1]

I cannot believe—I *refuse* to believe—that Magda Goebbels felt anything but love for her children. It was a fucked-up, warped sense of love, for sure, but love it was, nonetheless. Why else would they choose poison? They could easily have ordered a guard to shoot the children—instant death. Instead, Joseph instructed his dentist to administer large amounts of morphine to his six children so that they would lose consciousness. Then he and his wife crushed cyanide ampules in each of the children's mouths before he and Magda climbed out of their bunker, walked up to the garden of the Reich Chancellery, and together committed suicide.

In those final hours, Mr. and Mrs. Goebbels made some horrific choices. Those choices were made primarily out of fear for what would happen to them if they were to end up in the hands of their enemies. They were also made out of a misguided sense of loyalty and honor. But their choices were also made out of love.

Being in love and *falling* in love are things that happen to you. But *loving* someone is a choice. The choice to love someone also involves an enormous amount of vulnerability. Without vulnerability, you can neither be in love nor love someone else, not truly.

---

1 James Wyllie, *Nazi Wives: The Women at the Top of Hitler's Germany* (New York: St. Martin's Griffin, 2019), 223.

Because love is about giving someone the power to destroy you and trusting they won't use it. It is exactly that vulnerability to potentially being destroyed by someone else that acts as a glue between people who love each other.

And even though being in love is a chemically induced state of mind, it is by no means artificial. It is very real. Anyone who has experienced unrequited love or being dumped will understand this. Anyone who has lost a child will know just how real the pain of love can be. Joseph and Magda Goebbels knew that, if only for a few minutes. For a few minutes, they understood that love is also about pain and loss. Most human suffering is related to some kind of love or loss or both.

Oscar Wilde once quipped that one should always be in love, which is why one should never marry. There is more truth in Mr. Wilde's aphorism than I dare to admit. Anyone who has been in a long-term relationship knows exactly what I am talking about. Sharing your life with someone in such close quarters is difficult. It is also petrifying.

One thing that scares me is how often and how easily I have engaged in an argument with my wife, usually over things that we should not be arguing about at all, such as who does the most cleaning around the house or who takes most responsibility for the kids' schooling or who cooks the most.

And why shouldn't we be arguing over things like this? Simple. First of all, it makes no sense to argue with someone you love. And second, because my wife wins hands down in all the above categories.

Over time, I have discovered another aspect of my long-term relationship with my wife that also fills me with a deep sense of sadness and fear. It is the fact that, in my wife's universe, the kids come first. Always.

We can all be sitting at the dinner table having a family meal, and I can be telling her something about my day when suddenly, without prelude or warning, one of the children will start chirping away about something. It could be something important that needs immediate attention, like "I need a poo" or "My nose is bleeding." More often than not, though, it is something that could easily wait its turn, like "Why is poo always brown?" or "I did a somersault on the trampoline today!" Regardless of the importance of the chirping and regardless of whether it adds any value to the dinner table conversation—or to the cosmos in general—my wife's eyes will instantly go into screensaver mode. Her brain will shut down all radio frequencies related to her husband's words, and she will retune her antenna to the chirping and warbling of her kids.

"Yes, Christian, I did see your somersault on the trampoline today!"

"Yes, Emily, Rapunzel's hair was longer than yours."

"Yes, Olivia, Postman Pat's cat is definitely black and white."

Once she has dealt with the interruption—and only then—will she turn back to me, turn off her screensaver, tune in to my radio frequency again, and say, "Sorry, Pell, what were you saying?"

But by then, the moment is over. Besides, by the time my wife has redirected her attention to me, I am already drowning quietly in a maelstrom of rejection and resentment.

I know it sounds petty and trivial of me. I know that it is important to make our kids feel acknowledged and relevant in their interactions. I totally understand that kids find it difficult to hold back their instant urge to speak and that, as an adult man, I am much more psychologically equipped to deal with this rebuff, press the pause button, and wait for my turn again. I know all that. I get all that—intellectually, cognitively. However, those frequent, apparently insignificant snubs, when they become a part of the family dynamics, over many years, take an emotional toll.

And they create more distance between me and my wife. We pretend they don't, but they do. A sinister, almost imperceptible rift was forming between us, nothing more than a hairline fracture at first, but widening a millimeter or two every day. It's impossible to see the change from one day to another until it's too late; one day, you suddenly realize that you are standing on opposite sides of the Mid-Atlantic Ridge.

Out there in the animal world, alpha monkeys who feel ignored will often throw baby monkeys out of the tree and leave them for dead. Normally, it's the male that does this. His purpose is a simple and specific one: to get a female's undivided attention. And it works.

There is even one particular species of monkey—the moustached tamarin—where it is in fact the *mother* who carries out this atrocity. She does it to increase the odds of survival for the rest of the family when there is not enough food to go around or if sickness starts to spread within the group. There is no quarantine and social distancing for that unfortunate tamarin baby.

Sometimes, when the dirty deed has been done, the female moustached tamarin will even bite off the top of the baby's head and feed the protein-rich brain to the other babies to help keep them alive. How about that for an example of a positive intention behind a gruesome act? It makes the Goebbels look civilized in comparison.

I am ashamed to admit it, but on more than one occasion, I have wished that my wife was a moustached tamarin.

It's a wonder married couples bother to have children at all. In fact, it's a wonder married couples even bother to become couples, especially when you consider what the vast majority of couples will experience during their life together: Married couples will start families. They will argue about money. They will endure periods of boredom when life becomes a stream of routines, appointments, and deadlines, or "hectic monotony," as I call it. At some point, although they would never like to admit it, married couples will want to kill their kids too, just like moustached tamarins.

Or kill each other. I once heard of a married couple explain that their milestone sixty years together was explained by the fact that they had never wanted to divorce each other *at the same time*!

And then there is the sex. Or rather, and then there *isn't* the sex. The most frightening element of any long-term relationship is that, sooner or later, the original lust and passion you shared for one another will subside, and you will lose the desire to have sex with your partner as often as you did before. But why? Why should that once insatiable desire to be so intimately close to the person you love, the person you vowed to spend the rest of your life with, slowly but surely come to this erotic cul-de-sac?

Much of the explanation lies, I believe, in one of the cruelest paradoxes of love. The more you love a person and become familiar with them, the less you want to fuck them. And I use the word "fuck" here for a specific reason—not just to shock you. It is a cruel twist of cupid's dagger that the more you love a person, the less *in love* with them you become.

If you think back to the first time you enjoyed somebody else's body, the first time your body was entwined in carnal ecstasy with them, it was a time when you didn't really know that other person, at least not on a deep and personal level. There was a distance between you—not in physical terms, but in terms of familiarity. You didn't really know each other. It's the distance between people, the unchartered territory, that creates a sense of mystery. And with mystery comes adventure, risk, and desire.

It is precisely this distance that allows us to be erotic and sexual with the other person, that allows us to become someone or something our partner has not seen before. An animal perhaps? An animal of lust, even.

It's almost as if distance gives us permission to be someone else, to adopt another persona, and do things that we would not allow our public persona to do. When we adopt another persona, we can become a different character in our own sexual fantasies and live them out to the full in a sort of out-of-body experience.

But after living with someone for twenty years, you become too familiar with one another. You know all their habits, all their idiosyncrasies. You even know how their shit smells. You no longer have any mysteries or secrets. Very little, if anything, falls under the realm of fantasy anymore. The result is that this suffocates much of—if not all of—that which is erotic.

You need a sense of distance—even alienation—from the other person to really be erotic with them. Eroticism is not about closeness. Eroticism is about being able to create distance, if only for a little while.

CHAPTER 16

Being in Lust

I estimate that the distance between me and the woman sitting a few tables away in the frequent flyers lounge is five to six meters. It's far enough that I can observe her carefully and discreetly but not so far that I can't make out a few distinct details about her, like her watch. It is rose gold with diamonds around the face—elegant and upscale without being overly ostentatious. Her enameled fingernails are crimson. Her long hair is a dark honey blond, which perfectly complements her gray eyes.

Only 3 percent of the world's 8 billion people have gray eyes, something which makes her instantly more enigmatic and alluring. Plus, there are at least fifty shades of gray, which makes her even more unique. I decide to name her Miss Fifty Shades. I don't need to know her real name, though I do wonder which shade of gray she is.

I count how many breaths Miss Fifty Shades takes per minute, the number of times her full breasts rise and fall inside her dark business jacket: fourteen the first minute, sixteen the second.

Halfway through my third minute of counting, she looks up, as if she senses she is being watched. She doesn't glance directly at me, which is just as well, since the expression of boyish desire on my face would surely give me away, but she does start to scan her surroundings. She knows something is up.

Before her radar gets to me, I stand up and head for the buffet, which is conveniently situated outside her field of view. As I help myself to snacks at the lounge bar, I quietly admonish myself for my shady surveillance. I've always enjoyed people watching, which I consider to be a form of licit voyeurism. But this was more than that. This had furtive undertones. This was leering.

I press the button marked "Espresso" on the coffee machine. It's one of those machines that grinds your coffee for you while you wait for your drink, something that normally irritates me. I mean, would anyone really notice the difference in taste if they didn't hear the milling of coffee beans? Coffee experts will tell you that freshly ground coffee beans make for a more consistent flavor, though I wonder if your average airline passenger palate would pass the coffee equivalent of the Pepsi Challenge. I certainly wouldn't.

It's an obvious marketing ploy, and one that works extremely well, playing on the most evocative of the human senses—smell. Activating those olfactory and mirror neurons in us so that we actually believe that what we are about to drink has been hand ground and served, in person, by a Colombian coffee farmer.

Today, though, the extra time it takes to serve me my caffeine gives me a chance to gather myself before I return to my table. With any luck, by then Miss Fifty Shades will have left the lounge and headed off to her flight, so that I can refrain from being such a creepy voyeur.

And that's when it hits me. The bitter odor of ground coffee is replaced by the sweet scent of a woman's perfume, an aroma that perforates the back of my sinuses and fills them with sensual suggestion, a sensory overload of sultry summer gardenias and Amalfi Coast citrus groves tinged with the pungent aftertaste of honeysuckle and Irpinian juniper. The contrast between the sweet and bitter is what piques my senses. Like the espresso I am about to drink, it is bittersweet—just like my mother told me life should be. It's Miss Fifty Shades, I'm sure. I *want* it to come from her. I *want* her to still be here, still inside my orbit.

I turn around to see if my instincts are correct, picking up my coffee cup, trying to hold it steady in my unsteady hand. As I turn, I catch her eyes—not for too long but long enough to see that my instincts are right. It's her! I am also right about her eyes. They really are gray. And her hair really is dark honey blond. I am captivated by her, entranced, bewitched!

I move politely to one side to let Miss Fifty Shades select herself a cup of coffee. I stand as close to her as I dare, purposefully taking as long as possible to open a sachet of sugar and start pouring it into my coffee. As I watch the granules dropping into my coffee like an hourglass in slow motion, I inhale an extra deep breath of her perfume. Is it the juniper or the citrus that makes my heart start to beat a little faster?

By the time I get back to my table, her scent has dissipated into the air, and all that remains are the microscopic droplets that linger in the back of my throat. But she is definitely still in the room.

As I take my seat again, I waste no time going back to my clandestine ogling. On her way back from the coffee machine, I notice the heels on her shoes, though not stiletto, are pointy enough that they force her calves to tighten and flex all the way up to her skirt line, which is just above her knees. I dare not look any higher, though I am dying to confirm my suspicion that her legs are taut all the way up to her hips.

Her gait is one of poise, of feline agility and graceful noblesse. I am spellbound by the way she moves. Her hips slide gracefully and effortlessly into her chair. Any attempt I make now to stop my covert leering—and what I realize is little short of sexual harassment—would be futile. Her sensuality is magnetic, seductive, hypnotic. She's a Venus flytrap in an airline lounge, raising her coffee cup to her crimson lips to take a long and purposeful sip— long enough for me to see the ring on her finger. She's married.

So am I. They say that a man is only as faithful as his options, so I pick up my bags and head off to my gate, leaving behind a half-finished coffee and a half-told erotic storyline in my imagination.

. . .

My seat is 4F. It's always 4F. When you travel as much as I do, with as many as two hundred flights a year, you become a bit of a prima donna about certain things, like which seat you get, which types of nuts they serve on board, or how easily I can fly through the fast-track security line. And my seat has to be 4F, not

4A. Even though 4A is a window seat too, it's on the wrong side of the plane for a right-handed person like me, who doesn't want to be bumping elbows with the passenger in the middle seat. I need to keep my right hand free. And it must be the window, so that I can board early and lose myself in my book or my music or my thoughts, without having to pay attention to when someone needs me to stand up to let them get to *their* seat.

I look out my 4F window across at the neighboring gate, where travelers are making their way along the glass-walled boarding bridge and onto the plane. I spot Miss Fifty Shades boarding another flight; at least, I spot someone who I *think* is Miss Fifty Shades, but I soon realize that this woman's hair is more auburn than dark honey blond. Besides, her shoes have flat heels, her posture is too languid, her gait is too safe, too sober.

And that's when it hits me again, that smell: Amalfi citrus fruit, flowers, and juniper. Instinctively, I turn toward the source of the scent, to my left. She is there, sitting right beside me.

She throws me a courtesy smile, the kind that frequent travelers do to acknowledge each other's presence. She places her handbag underneath the seat in front of her and starts to remove her overcoat, her lithe body effortlessly sliding it off her shoulders and pulling it around her body. She hangs it up on the hook behind the seat of the passenger in front and settles down to read her magazine.

Her right wrist is just centimeters away from mine, close enough for me to count the number of diamonds around the watch face. It's a Rolex Lady-Datejust 36. The number 36 denotes the diameter of the watch face in millimeters, the perfect size for her slender arms.

She wears the watch on her right arm. I wear mine on my left, the more common option since most people are right-handed. She must be left-handed, I conclude. I learned from Titch McCarthy in his Latin class that *sinistra* was the Latin word for "the left hand"—as it is in modern Italian too—and that the left-hand side was considered to be the side of bad omens, hence the word *sinister*. It was said that the devil himself was left-handed.

I fill my lungs with her perfume, savoring her pheromones, delighting in the lust she ignites in me. If only she knew the effect that she was having on me. If only I were bold enough to tell her or brazen enough to reach out and caress the back of her hand!

But I am not that person. So, instead, I make do with having my hand as close to hers as I dare, our watches so close to each other that I am sure I can sense some static electricity between them, like two Van de Graaf generators.

As we near the end of our short flight, one of the cabin attendants leans in to signal that he would like to take my food tray. I lift it up and start to hand it back to him.

Miss Fifty Shades looks up, smiles, and without hesitation helps guide my tray over her seat toward the flight attendant. As she does this, our watches accidentally collide with a soft clink.

"Oh, sorry!" we say simultaneously.

This is my cue, the perfect excuse to open a conversation with her. Any line would do, even a corny one like, "Whoops! It would be such a shame to damage such a nice watch; I hope I didn't scratch it," or just "Nice watch, by the way." And then she could return the compliment by saying, "Likewise."

My Panerai watch may not be as bling as hers, but anyone who wears a watch like hers must know *something* about watches. She might even know that the people who hand built my watch come from a long line of Florentine watchmakers dating back to 1860, that, today, Panerai makes its watches in Switzerland, combining the style of Italy with the precision of Switzerland.

We could then exchange views about how wonderful it is to be the owner of a luxury watch, not just because of its value or status, but because a hand-built watch is organic and analogue—no need to charge it at night, no need for software updates, no error messages. It lives its own self-winding life, a comforting contrast to the digital world we live in.

I could tell her how I'd never even owned a proper watch until I turned fifty-two and literally, one day, just decided to go out and buy myself a midlife crisis present. I could recount how surprised I was that I became so quickly attached to my Italian–Swiss piece. Yes, it's a *piece*, not a *watch*; that's what the Panerai Service Center called it when I spoke to them once. A thirty-minute call, and not once did the service person call it a watch. And we would tell each other that we would keep our pieces for life. I mean, how many things last a lifetime anymore?

Tattoos perhaps, I could suggest.

Certainly not relationships, she could reply.

And then we'd segue into relationships, and, well, you know how the rest plays out.

But my heart is beating way too fast. I am just not that brazen or bold, not that audacious in my approach to women. I never have been. So, I chicken out and return to the view outside the window of seat number 4F. *Probably for the best*, I think. I know it's in my genes, but there is no need to pull the trigger. No need to force this situation down a dead-end, sinister avenue.

That would have been the end of that little not-so-innocent encounter had I not seen her standing in front of me at the hotel check-in desk. *Perhaps she is attending the same conference as me tomorrow.* It is impossible to ignore my own heartbeat hammering away at my Adam's apple. Had Eve offered me an apple right now, I would have devoured it!

We are standing in the lift together. Did she actually wait for me to check in before she summoned the lift? Surely not. We exchange pleasantries, confirm what time the conference begins. She *is* going to the same event, which means she'll be watching me when I stand on the main stage, giving my keynote in the morning.

"Nice watch," she says.

"Likewise," I reply.

That's your cue, I tell myself. *Tattoos and relationships! Go for it!*

Her room card number is as easy to read as her watch now. Sorry, her *piece*.

I make no effort to hide my own room card. I make sure to hold it in my left hand too, the hand of the devil.

She leaves the lift on the third floor, her perfume leaving behind her a vortex of temptation and enticement, tinged with the pungent aftertaste of honeysuckle and juniper. I am sure her scent will still be hanging in the air in the morning when I come down for breakfast.

I leave the lift on the fourth floor, leaving behind me a trail of unrequited sin. As I close the door behind me, I am grateful that I make it to the sanctuary of my room alone, without having committed any indiscretion. I even congratulate myself for overriding my genetic programming, for ending that scene. My genetic gun has definitely been loaded; I sensed it deep in the marrow of my bones. But I refrained from pulling the trigger. Environment has not had the final say, not this time.

I can relax; I am safe. The next test will come tomorrow, when I meet her again at the conference. But that's tomorrow. For now, sleep awaits, and I am only too happy to fall into her gentle arms.

But not long after I switch off the bedside lamp, I hear a soft knocking on my door. I lie still. Perhaps it came from the room above me or the room next door.

Knock, knock, it comes again. This time, there is no mistaking that the knocking is on my door.

I pull away my bed covers and walk slowly toward it. Slowly and deliberately, I open the door.

It's her. Miss Fifty Shades.

· · ·

I would like to be able to tell you that I resisted. I would love to be able to tell you that I politely sent Miss Fifty Shades back to her room like a good *Homo sapiens* should, would, and could.

After all, *sapiens* does mean wise, and that is exactly what a wise, rational, logical human being would do, right?

But, you know, when Robin Williams bluntly and brazenly quipped once that God gave man a penis and a brain but only enough blood to run one at a time, he communicated more wisdom and insight in that one line than any of my teachers at school ever did, Titch McCarthy included.

So I open the door and invite Miss Fifty Shades into my room.

We have not said a word to each other yet. There is no need. It is already abundantly clear that we are beyond the point of no return, past any pretense or pleasantries. The most ridiculous and inauthentic thing I could say now would be "How can I help you?" or "I think you've got the wrong room." We dispensed with our courtship and flirting in the lounge, in seats 4E and 4F, and in the hotel lift.

It's obvious why she is here. There is nothing subtle about her intentions, something that is accentuated by the fact that she has discarded both her watch and her ring—no deadlines, no commitments. She has also left behind her jacket, revealing the full splendor of her breasts, which swell behind her thin scoop-neck top.

My eyes are scanning her up and down, just like I did at the airport lounge. Only then, I was more subtle. Now that there are no casual bystanders and potential whistleblowers, I am free to size her up much more avidly, more hungrily.

She welcomes my scrutiny with lascivious eyes. She *wants* me to size her up. She can see that her proportions are instantly appealing to me—captivating, bewitching. What, perhaps, she doesn't know is that her proportions are a near-perfect zero point seven. According to a number of experts, divide a woman's waist size by her hip size, and if the answer is 0.7, the primeval male mind subconsciously concludes *good hormone balance, good resistance to disease, good fertility, good potential mate, inseminate her!*

It doesn't matter how large or small the waist and hips are either, as long as the final ratio is 0.7. It doesn't matter if your name is Marilyn Monroe or Twiggy, Sophia Loren or Kate Moss, Scarlett Johansson, or Kim Kardashian. Just as long as the calculation generates a result of 0.7—or within a decimal point or two; the male brain is not *that* precise or picky—men will look at you and subconsciously come to the same conclusion: I want to inseminate you!

This is why Barbie dolls are not only completely unrealistic and unfeasible but also very unattractive. At least to grown fertile men they are. If Barbie were a real woman, she would have a hip-to-waist ratio of less than 0.5, which basically communicates to the average male that Barbie Woman's hormone balance is askew. She is more than likely to fall ill a lot, she will be difficult to get pregnant, and she will probably spend most of her time either starving herself or puking her food back up after ingesting it. In other words, Barbie Woman would be a bulimic, infertile, hypochondriac. No point fucking her then, concludes the average male.

What's more, her sixteen-inch waist would be four inches thinner than her head, which would mean that Barbie Woman would only have enough room for half a liver and a few inches of intestines! This would make going to a simple dinner party very challenging and decidedly unglamorous, since the alcohol and sugar of a simple cocktail would wreak havoc on her under-size liver.

Also, since she would have the intestinal tract of a South-east-Asian tree shrew, the minute she finishes eating her *hors d'oeuvre* she would be heading for the shitter. And as if that weren't enough to turn you off, her bamboo-like neck and lollipop-stick ankles would be too thin to support her head, so she would end up crawling around the house on all fours, her head resting on top of a tea trolley!

Barbie dolls are a complete figment of a fucked-up imagination, and there is nothing glamourous or dream-like about the life of a Barbie doll. Miss Fifty Shades, on the other hand, is no Barbie doll. Miss Fifty Shades is what *real* dreams are made of.

And here she is, standing right in front of me, the distance between us so small now that I can detect alcohol on her breath. I don't know if "distance" is the right word to use, though. "Gap" is better, perhaps. Yes, gap. Mind the gap! Oh, I am minding the gap, all right, tantalizingly, teasingly minding the gap, my toes balancing precariously on the edge of the platform, the sliding doors just a step away, my body acutely aware of the consequences of taking one step forward into the abyss, one leap of faith into the arms of another unfaithful sinner.

"Why me?" I ask.

"I've seen you before," she answers. "You were on stage at a conference I attended in Trondheim."

"Trondheim?" I ask her, feigning curiosity but really just trying to buy myself some time while I summon up the courage to do what I want, even though it may not be what I need—to step off the ledge and fall into the arms of fate. I wasn't able to go through with it at Preikestolen, but perhaps I can muster up enough spunk now. The sliding doors await—just one step.

"I was sitting in the audience about five rows back from the stage, to your left. I was about to leave actually. I wasn't really getting anything out of the event. I'd heard most of it before. And then the conference host suddenly announced your name. I'd never heard a name like that before. And the way you walked onto the stage—so confident, so self-assured, so anchored. I just thought, *Wow, who is this?*"

She throws me a mischievous, wanton smile and takes half a step toward me. I am still minding the gap, though—what little gap there is left, that is.

"Did you like the presentation?" I ask, and immediately cringe at my own question.

What a ridiculous thing to say! What a turn-off! I've obviously not done this kind of thing before. This is something I am definitely not so self-assured about. I love that she describes me as being anchored, but to be honest, right now my anchor feels like it is being dragged aimlessly and recklessly along a muddy riverbed. I am deflecting her words of seduction. I don't know why. There's absolutely no need to. All I have to do now is walk through the door.

"I loved it!" she sighs, her alcohol-laced breath caressing my nostrils again, this time with more force, more potency. Perhaps it's the alcohol that makes her so assertive, so candid. "Although I don't remember much of what you said," she adds. "No offense."

"None taken," I reply, hoping that my quizzical expression doesn't betray that I actually have.

"What I *do* remember, though," she continues, "is thinking after just a few minutes, *Wow, what a man!*"

"What a man?" My face transforms into a question mark.

"Yes, what a man!" she replies. "A *real* man!"

Her answer startles me, surprises me, catches me off guard. It's corny. It's a cliché of porn-like proportions, but her line sends a torrent of testosterone gushing through my veins and down to my pelvis. But the testosterone is laced with skepticism and self-doubt, the same sensation a midlife-crisis man gets when he plucks up the courage to look at himself in the mirror after he's stepped out of the shower. I have to say that I can't even remember the last time I did that. But this mirror makes me eager to deactivate all my bullshit filters—anything to help me get the attention and validation I so desperately need.

"A man has only one escape from his old self," wrote the playwright and activist Clare Boothe Luce, "and that is to see a different self in the mirror of some woman's eyes." That mirror is standing right before me in a fourth-floor hotel room. This explains why I am gullible enough to gobble up her pickup lines, her ruse, even though I know, deep down inside, that I am certainly not that real man she thinks she is seeing.

How could I be? All the evidence she has to go on is that one performance on stage in Trondheim. She doesn't know me at all.

She can only see my outer layer, the man whose persona is exaggerated and glorified whenever he steps out onto a stage in front of hundreds of people, bathed in soft stage lighting and audience applause. But once I step off that stage, I become the same as so many other middle-aged men, drowning quietly in all his flaws and uncertainties. She has no idea that behind this competent exterior lurks a very incompetent interior. She has no inkling that before her now stands a man who, for the most part, fires blanks, whose sperm quality has officially been archived on the Andrology Centre server as *very poor*. Blind, directionless, retarded sperm. Not even her perfect hip-to-waist ratio could change that.

Would she think I was a real man if she'd seen me in a pair of white lady-slippers, shuffling along a linoleum corridor toward a masturbatorium to watch hairy Hungarian porn stars fucking each other? I don't think so. And what would Miss Fifty Shades think if she knew that my Iron Crotch Qi Gong hard-on was down to a double dose of blue diamonds? Or if she knew that I had watched my own mother get dragged across a kitchen floor by her hair, her face dripping San Marzano pasta sauce, screaming for help, while I just sat there and did nothing? Or that I let my three-year-old daughter walk into a swimming pool on her own?

"What's wrong?" she asks. "You look nervous."

She doesn't *ask* me if I'm nervous. She *tells* me that I am nervous. She is so confident, so forthright, so sure of herself. Where has this woman come from? I've never met a woman like this before.

"Don't be nervous," she reassures me. "Nobody will know. Nobody will see. I'm married too."

"Yes, I saw that. What happened to your ring? And your watch?"

"No deadlines, no commitments, right?" She smiles.

"Did you just say, 'No deadlines, no commitments'?"

"Isn't that what you were thinking when you opened the door?"

"I was. . . . But how did you . . . ? When did you . . . ?"

Her extrasensory perception startles me, sends me back half a step, back to minding my gap, eyeing this woman with suspicion, this clairvoyant, this *bruja*.

A word I still remember from when I was teaching English in Spain in the mid-1980s, *bruja* means "witch." People used it in the expression "¡Qué bruja eres!" (What a witch you are!). You would say it to someone who displayed great intuition or who was clever or cunning or just tuned in to other people's vibes. You would only use it with someone you knew well, and you would say it in a playful way, with a glint in your eye. In the right context, with the appropriate amount of irony and good nature, it would be considered a compliment. You would never be able to get away with it in English or Italian.

"¡Qué bruja eres!" I whisper. My words are hardly perceptible, even in the silence of my hotel room.

"Maybe."

Her one-word response startles me even more. It strikes me in the chest like a wrecking ball. Thud!

"'A vita è bella, pure quanno è brutta, Miss Fifty Shades," I mumble under my breath. Am I about to have one of those *bella-brutta* moments with Miss Fifty Shades?

"Maybe," she replies again.

Her body smells of citrus flowers and junipers and her breath of sweet alcohol. My God! That smell! It smells the same as my mother's breath on Christmas Day. My mother loved her Strega, the drink of witches, best drunk with the hand of the devil, no doubt.

"Don't be scared. Nobody will know. Nobody will get hurt. What matters is this, right here, right now."

And then we kiss. Carefully. Purposefully. My tongue is soon drenched in her Strega-spiked saliva.

Instinctively, I reach around her slender 0.7-ratio waist and hips, softly grabbing her buttocks, my fingers already groping for the lower part of her butt. With both hands, I pull her hips toward mine, my arousal unmistakable. Her arms reach up and around my neck as she increases the intensity of her kiss, her left leg already making its way up and around my thigh, like an anaconda encircling its prey, ready to squeeze the life from it.

The hemline of her skirt rises upward toward her panties, which I am sure will be deliciously elegant once they are fully revealed. I make a mental note to remove them as delicately as they were put on in the first place.

As she snakes her limbs around me, I begin to feel the full weight of her body pulling down on my neck, our hips stuck to one another like electromagnets, lactic acid building up in my thigh muscles. I give in to the force and drop with her down onto the bed, our mouths releasing from each other for the first time. As she is lain out below me, my right knee placed firmly between her thighs, she lets her arms fall above her head, outstretched, as if to emphasize her submission to me.

"I want you!" I hiss. And I *do* want her. Badly. I need her too, but it's not the need that drives my desire; it's the want.

"It's time!" she hisses back, opening both her lips and her legs in dual anticipation.

There's an awful lot of hissing going on right now, I think. None of those hairy Hungarian porn actors at the Andrology Centre hissed. They just moaned and groaned.

"Now, you owe your lover a service," she says, still hissing.

"Did you just say, 'You owe your lover a service?'" I ask my hissing seducer. "Where have I heard that before? Shouldn't it be you owe your *Don* a service? Yes, of course, *Godfather 1*, when Tom Hagen calls the undertaker to arrange Sonny's funeral."

"No, you owe your *lover* a service," she insists, hissing even louder.

"Could you stop hissing, please?" I ask her. "It's about as sexually arousing as the hiss of a slow puncture."

Miss Fifty Shades ignores my request and whispers back, "She has no doubt that you will repay her."

And we're back to *The Godfather* again. Another jolt. Another wrecking ball thud in my chest. Another sensory hijack. Where does she get all these words from? Not only can she read my thoughts; she can read my memories! But how? This is all so flamboyantly illogical, so disinhibited, and so wonderfully liberating!

All of a sudden, it feels like I've been granted access to another version of myself that I had long thought dead. But that version of me will only truly reveal itself if I allow myself to step outside the comfort zone of rule-abiding convention. I need my prefrontal cortex to go offline so that I can walk through that sliding door, so that I can free myself to indulge in these flamboyantly illogical acts, these outbursts of emotion, and these spasms of hypersexuality. But once I do choose to walk through that door, I can never go back. It's an exciting proposition but also one that will leave a blemish on my soul for all eternity.

Desire is about adventure, novelty, mystery. It is about danger, and risk, the forbidden fruit. No wonder affairs are so appealing to the human spirit. Responsibility—marriage, a family—and desire simply do not belong together. People talk about being happily married, but how many couples have you heard tell you that they are *passionately* married?

"What are you waiting for?" she asks with a gentle writhing of her hips.

What *am* I waiting for? Here I am, like a Magnum .44, cocked, locked, and ready to rock, my mirror neurons buzzing with anticipation as I visualize what I am about to do *to* and *with* her. Professor Giacomo Rizzolatti would have nodded in approval right now.

Miss Fifty Shades looks robust enough to take the brute force that I am about to unleash on her, the violence and abandon with which I am about to ravage and consume her. She has awakened a man inside me that I haven't seen for years, a man I thought had been erased from my internal hard drive years ago—a sleeping giant, a powerhouse of raw animal lust. He is rough. He is burly. And he is aggressive. He is a real man. He doesn't want to make sweet love to her. He wants to *take* her. And that is exactly what she wants him to do to her. This is her fantasy too. I am sure of it.

"It's okay. You can be yourself with me," she whispers again. "I want you with all your flaws, with all your violence, and anger, and regret . . . everything that makes you the man you are. In sickness and in health. 'Til my death do us part."

"Huh? What did you say?"

This time, the wrecking ball thud in my chest jolts me out of my hypnotic reverie. *'Til my death do us part? Your death? Why* your *death?*

But before I can process her words, she hisses once more, "I want you!" and pulls me down into the depths of our mutual bliss. She contracts her serpentine muscular body once more in lateral undulation over the bed, teasing her skirt even higher up her hips to reveal light blue silk panties.

Just as I thought—deliciously elegant.

My eyes move up to her exposed navel—perfectly round and perfectly centered. It's too perfect, perhaps, as if it has been photoshopped and airbrushed for a Hollywood movie poster. But not too perfect that I cannot kiss it and lick it. I lean into her toned stomach and savor her perspiring body with the tip of my tongue. Salty.

She moans softly, stretching her arms even farther toward the headboard, her scoop-neck top unable to contain her breasts anymore.

Instinctively, I move my mouth upward in search of more erogenous zones.

"I'm hot!" she purrs. "I need to take my top off."

"Yes, do that!"

"You do it!" And with that, she stretches her arms out again above her head.

That's when I notice something very odd. The sweat patches under her arms are unusually large for a woman. They are much larger even than the ones I get when I am on a big stage in front of hundreds of expectant audience members, and I am probably almost twice her size and weight.

I also realize I don't even know her name. It has never crossed my mind until now to even ask. Then again, I haven't needed to know her name. Miss Fifty Shades works just fine. In fact, not knowing her name is probably advisable, considering what I am about to do with her. It'll be less incriminating. But now it feels like I need to ask, like it's the polite thing to do. After all, I have just licked her salty navel and tasted her Strega breath.

"Before I take your top off, I need to know one thing."

"Don't worry," she replies. "Nobody will find out. I have as much to lose as you do. I won't tell a soul. It will be as if this never happened."

"No, it's not that."

"What then? What is it? Ask me."

"What is your name?"

As she opens her mouth to answer, the sweat patches on her scoop-neck top turn from misty gray to blue, silky blue, arctic blue. And she starts to move in slow motion.

Why is she moving in slow motion? I'm not.

In what seems like an instant but takes an eternity, her entire top becomes drenched in blue fluid, her skirt, her deliciously elegant panties, her airbrushed navel drowning in this azure solution. And now she's sinking into the bed, her mane of tangled honey blond hair dragging her down like heavy seaweed. Her arms reach out for me, pleading with me to save her from drowning in the depths of her despair. And all I can do is scream out my question again.

"What is your name? *Your name!*"

. . .

I pull myself up from my pillow to a seated position, like an airline seat just before landing—only this time there is no scent of a woman beside me. I am covered in sweat. The room is pitch black, or maybe my eyes are still closed. In this hypnagogic state, I find it difficult to distinguish fact from fiction, so I stretch my hand—my olive branch hand—out into the dark hotel room, back into my dream, back into my memory. But it doesn't reach. I can still see her sinking, sinking into the blue water. The last part of her to disappear is her mouth. Her tasty, succulent mouth with those luscious crimson lips and spiced alcohol breath.

And then her crimson lips also fade to blue. Everything is so blue, silky blue. Everything except the multicolored *mo-say-ick* behind her. And as the waters around her prepare to consume her for good, I plead to her one more time.

"Your name! Please tell me your name."

Her response is one, simple, Strega-laced word: "Olivia."

CHAPTER 17

Are You Lonesome Tonight?

The next morning, I wake up alone. I shower, get dressed, and go down to the hotel restaurant for my breakfast. Alone. After I check my presentation with the technical staff at the conference venue, I retire to a corner of the auditorium, find myself a chair, and sit down. Alone. Just like I always do.

I like being on my own. It's a common misconception that public speakers are all extroverts, in constant need of being surrounded by lots of people. I am comfortable standing on a stage and talking to large crowds, but once I am away from that limelight, I am more than happy to stay there.

Many introverts create a barrier between themselves and the rest of the world, a way to protect themselves from others. For speakers, this can be a podium or even the stage itself, but it's often more metaphorical. My barrier today is the space between my little chair in the corner of the auditorium and the audience.

This is where I like to watch and listen to the other speakers and participants—just me, alone, in quiet solitude.

Today is different, though. Today, I am not only alone; I am lonely. There is a big difference between solitude and loneliness. Solitude is a choice. Loneliness is most definitely not. Solitude is the joy of being alone. Loneliness is the *pain* of being alone. Right now, I am in pain.

I am in pain because, last night, I did something I should not have done. Even if it was only in my dreams, it feels exactly as if I'd done it in real life. Professor Giacomo Rizzolatti was right: I am just like that monkey that watched his little simian friend munch peanuts. My brain doesn't know the difference. My mirror neurons don't lie. As far as my brain is concerned, I have committed adultery.

This is all the more remarkable because, when we sleep, our brain blocks out all sensory perceptions, which is why we enter a state of atonia—or paralysis. Gently lift up the arm of a child when she is fast asleep, and you can feel just how limp and "lifeless" her arm is. There are literally no electrical impulses going through that arm—no tension, no resistance. If that arm were not warm to the touch, you would think you were actually holding the arm of a corpse.

Even though I was in a state of paralysis last night as I slept and dreamt about Miss Fifty Shades, my brain believes 100 percent that it did the dirty deed. And if my brain feels that, then so do I feel that.

But I was not alone; I was doing it with someone. I was able to forget some of the pain of my loneliness because I was sharing something significant with someone—a fantasy, sure, but she was real enough to my mirror neurons. My infidelity served as a welcome balm for my loneliness. It is easy to understand why the number-one reason people have affairs is loneliness.

Loneliness is not only about the physical absence of other people. It's the sense that you're not sharing anything that matters with anyone else. It's the feeling you get when you have just heard the best joke, and you have nobody to tell it to, nobody to spread the joy to. Loneliness is a malady, a sickness. It is not just a state of mind; it is something you suffer from, like cancer. And it is almost as deadly as cancer too. I know this because the first speaker on stage is talking about this very topic.

"Studies have shown that obesity increases the likelihood of an early death by 20 percent, excessive drinking by 30 percent," the speaker informs the audience.

A quiet murmur spreads through the audience, no doubt initiated by those who were planning to hit the conference bar immediately after the daytime sessions are over to get a head start on the conference's social event later that evening.

"Loneliness increases the chances of premature death by a staggering"—she leaves the words hanging in the air for a beat, before bringing up the next slide of her presentation, which has one single number on it—"45 percent."

A respectful, somber silence falls over the auditorium. A number of people lift their gaze and check out the number on the screen.

"I see a number of you are looking away from your phones," continues the speaker. "That's good. Because psychologists use terms like *the paradox of social media* and *alone together*."

Alone together—that's what I was last night, I think. Alone together. I was with Miss Fifty Shades, but I was on my own.

"Overuse and overreliance on social media for our personal connections does not make you feel more connected with people at all, but the exact opposite," she continues. She knows she has the audience's full attention now.

"Social media often leads to a state of chronic loneliness. The physical and mental health aspect of chronic loneliness is a public health issue that now rivals cancer and heart disease."

And angst, I say to myself. My thoughts wander back to the time I stood on top of Preikestolen and contemplated the unthinkable. When I remembered all those places in Norway that had the word *anger* in them—Geiranger, Hardanger, Levanger, Høyanger, Varanger, Orkanger, Bremanger, Kaupanger.

Last night was wonderful. But it was also full of regret and angst. And ultimately, loneliness.

When you are suffering from loneliness, people say the strangest things to you: *You should get out more. You should join a sports club. How do you expect to make friends if you don't make the effort?* All of these things have been said to me—and, for sure, to others who have felt lonely. Logically, they make sense, I suppose. But emotionally, psychologically, they mean nothing. The worst one I heard was "Nobody can help you except yourself."

Let me explain why this is such a ridiculous thing to say. When I have been in the darkest depths of my loneliness and isolation, it feels like I've been subjected to an unprovoked attack in the middle of the city in broad daylight. I am laid out on the ground, semiconscious, paralyzed, bleeding. I can make out voices around me, faces even, but none of them are looking at me or talking about me. There are no good Samaritans around today. Nobody is coming up to help me to see if I am all right.

Imagine you happen to be passing by and see me lying there. You walk up to me, lean down and whisper sympathetically into my ear, "You should get out more. Nobody can help you except yourself."

When you are locked in loneliness, nobody comes to help. Nobody reaches out a hand and invites you gently into their world. Eventually, loneliness becomes a deceptive filter through which we see both ourselves and the world around us. This filter makes us more vulnerable to rejection, it makes us more suspicious of others, and it magnifies our levels of vigilance and insecurity in social situations. The pain of this state of mind is often unbearable.

Miss Fifty Shades was different. She did the exact opposite of what most people do. She came to *me*. She broke the pattern. *She* made the first move. If only she had been real and not just a figment of my mirror neurons.

Miss Fifty Shades made me feel as if I was somebody, a real man. In her eyes, I was desirable. I was sensual. Dammit, I was sexy! Not because of what she did to me, not because of the sensations she stirred up in me, but because of the *ideas* she instilled in me—most of all, acceptance for who I am and the promise of an end to loneliness and shame. Miss Fifty Shades had brought down the three pillars of loneliness that had been my foundation for far too long—separation, shame, and fear. Miss Fifty Shades was my Samson, and I was her Delilah.

I know that my sexual desire for her was driven by the anxiety of loneliness. I could have stopped it. But I didn't. When I opened the hotel room door to her—even though she wasn't real—I allowed myself to become completely self-absorbed. Suddenly, everything became about me. Call it vanity, call it selfishness, call it narcissism. Call it what you like. I don't really care. All I know is that there and then, in that moment, I was lovable again.

Dreams are not a replay of our waking day. They are not recordings. If all they did was replay us our day, dreams would be really drab and lacking in fantasy and vibrancy. Dreams are an unconscious state in which we fulfill our repressed wishes. They also help us sort out our emotional lives, especially our worries, concerns, shortcomings, and fears. Dreams nurse our emotional and mental health. They also provide clues about how to solve those problems and in which direction to apply our solutions. Miss Fifty Shades provided me with a sense of direction. She was the catalyst I needed to embark on a mission to feel good about myself again. She was my ticket to ride. She was my way out of the narrow, constricted fjord of *anger*. Norwegian Anger.

But in the end, she was also a nightmarish reminder of my greatest failure. Was it loneliness Olivia felt that day, or was it solitude? As she descended into the clear waters of that pool, was she brimming with the joy of solitude, or was she filled with the *pain* of being alone?

I need to believe that it was solitude. I need to believe that, in those eighteen seconds before the water would start to fill her lungs, at least her *heart* was filled with the joy of a solo adventurer toward that scintillating secret at the bottom of the pool, that *mo-say-ick*.

. . .

They say that there is nothing worse than dying alone. Facedown on a hospital bed, attached to a respirator as some virus ravages your body. Those final moments before the palliative stupor of the morphine kicks in. The sense of helplessness of your family and friends, who are unable to hold you and comfort you in your final hour. The overwhelming weight of regret for all the things they wish they could have said to you before you died. So many things.

Or facedown in the snow, stuck on a Himalayan limestone alcove with your green boots poking out of the snow. You know that every one of your fellow climbers wanted to come and help you, but at over eight thousand meters in the oxygen-starved "Death Zone," any attempts at rescue would have meant certain death for them too. So they had to leave you there, half buried in drifting snow, with your green boots sticking out like some eerie warning beacon. Sleep well, Green Boots. Sleep in peace.

In my sleep, I have nightmares about dying alone in a hotel room—or on the toilet. Apparently, many people draw their last breath while straining on the loo. Push a little too hard and your blood pressure increases so much that it can cause a heart attack or an aneurysm. That's how Elvis died: the king alone on his porcelain throne. Are you lonesome tonight, Mr. Presley?

Since I spend about a third of my year sleeping in hotels and going to the bathroom in them, neither one of these sad curtain calls is completely improbable. If that is the way I am going to go, then I already feel sorry for the poor cleaning staff who will probably be the ones to find me.

She's probably called Agnieszka or Sheela or Onyechi. She'll knock on my door, which I won't hear because I'm dead. She'll walk into my room, perhaps calling out a courtesy "Room service!" as her eyes adjust to the darkness. She may even think, *What the hell is this guy doing? It's way past checkout time, and I've got shitloads of rooms to finish cleaning before I can call it a day.* She'll switch on the light, and—boom!—an eyeful of hairy arsehole and droopy man bits.

This is why I always keep my underpants on when I sleep in a hotel. You know, just in case.

Perhaps this is why my subconscious chose a hotel room for Miss Fifty Shades to come to me, the one place it knew I would be at my most solitary, my most vulnerable, or, as Elvis would put it, at my most lonesome.

I also wear my watch to bed—sorry, my *piece*. Former Norwegian TV2 boss Kåre Valebrokk once said that being found dead with a cheap watch on your wrist is even worse than being found dead in dirty underpants. I agree with him. I must admit it does provide me with *some* comfort to know that the paramedic administering CPR on me says something like, "I don't think he's going to make it, but hey, check out his watch, man!"

My mother died alone. Not on the toilet, thankfully, but in the kitchen. A sudden heart attack brought her crashing down to the kitchen floor. The paramedics later told us that she'd died instantly. She didn't even have time to put her arms out to break her fall. She certainly couldn't have had time to tell herself that life was beautiful even when it's ugly. When you die at the age of forty-two, there are probably many things you feel you didn't have time for.

It was a chilly, rainy Monday morning in late October 1981. Half-term holidays—no Derek to worry about, no pugilistic Titch McCarthy to facilitate and augment my erudition, no Om to ask if he could come over here a minute and turn on a tap for us weaklings. Again, Om, I am so sorry.

I didn't hear the angels on that Monday morning either. I was awake, but since the weather outside was so uninviting, I had decided to stay a little longer in bed and listen to some music. I had to do this with headphones because my father had just put his head down after his first night of yet another week of night shifts. No half term for him. I'd just bought an album by Rush called *Moving Pictures*. Seven wonderful tracks hot off the press. I was focusing on learning Neil Peart's latest drum licks and fills, which was not an easy task, I can tell you. I idolized The Professor, as he was known, and tried to emulate him in my own playing. I remember how I would terrorize my fellow classmates at St. Brendan's by playing the drums to entire Rush songs on my desk with my fingers—the same desks that many of our caring Catholic cunt teachers like Derek used to bludgeon our palms on in penance.

On that Monday morning, I was busy trying to learn as many drum licks and drum fills as possible so that I could do my air drumming properly at the Rush concert I had managed to get tickets for at Bingley Hall in Stafford on October 29. I only had three days to practice.

As I lay there in bed listening, studying Peart's idiosyncratic time signatures, my mother was downstairs boiling an egg for my baby brother, who was two years old at the time. I was seventeen. I like to explain that the age gap between us was the result of a bodily reconciliation between my mother and my father after the salt episode. Oh, the stories we concoct for ourselves just to make life more palatable!

The next thing I knew, my brother was standing beside me, tugging on my pajama sleeve. Even with all the language limitations of a two-year-old, I had no difficulty understanding that he wanted me to come downstairs. The look of confusion and bewilderment in his eyes told me that I should do it quickly, too.

It's a wonderfully unique quality we humans have, the ability to communicate volumes through the whites of our eyes—the sclera, to give them their proper name. While the vast majority of other animals and mammals have either a dark sclera or a narrow one, human eyes have evolved in the opposite direction, with visible, wide bands of white around the iris. The reason why animals have a dark sclera—especially predators—is so that they can conceal both themselves and their intentions from their prey. The last thing a prowling panther in the night needs is a pair of bright white eyeballs to light him up as he stalks his next meal.

We humans are not predators or prowlers by nature. We are group-oriented hunter-gatherers, where group cohesion and a cooperative mindset have proven invaluable in our fight for survival. Letting as many people around you as possible know *exactly* what you're thinking makes it easier for others to trust you. The larger the sclera, the more communicative we become, even when no words come out of our mouths. Also, the larger the sclera, the more transparent and revealing we become of our intentions and emotions, and so the greater the sense of trust we create with others. This is why people who *don't* want to reveal what they are thinking or feeling often wear dark sunglasses, like champion poker players, secret agents, or cyborg terminators.

On that Monday morning in 1981, my brother's scleras were as white and wide as could be.

I threw off my headphones and cast them down on to the floor, Neil Peart's drumbeats still pounding out of the spongy earpieces. As I made my way down the stairs, I caught the smell of something burning. I hit the bottom of the stairs, turned toward the kitchen, and immediately noticed smoke seeping out from under the door—a rancid, light-colored smoke, like the cigarette smoke that used to find its way out from behind the bathroom door when my mother sneaked off to steal a few puffs.

As I pushed the kitchen door open, the full impact of the frazzled egg in the pan hit me. How long did it take for boiling water in a saucepan to evaporate away? Twenty minutes? Thirty? The egg had already been burnt to a crisp, and black smoke filled the kitchen.

I found her on the kitchen floor, her eyes slightly open. A small trickle of blood ran from her left nostril, the only telltale sign of a fall. I was the one who called the ambulance. I remember that. But after that, I remember little, at least right up to the point when the paramedics took her away. By then, I had retreated back to my bedroom. I don't know why. I didn't want my lasting memory of her to be her being carried out on a stretcher, I guess, and I was already erasing the image of her on the kitchen floor from my brain's hard disk.

No, I wanted my lasting memories of her to be the smell of the chamomile tea she made me in the evenings before bedtime. I wanted to remember her telling me stories of angels and witches, even her calling me Pelli instead of Pell.

I'd left my bedroom door slightly open so I could hear the inconsolable commotion downstairs in the hallway. I could hear my father weeping over my mother. The paramedics were ready to leave. To them, this was just another emergency response of a seemingly endless list of distress calls. And yet, they stood there for a few moments, holding the stretcher with my mother on it, so that my father and my sister could bid her a final farewell while there was still *some* warmth in her body. I imagined she just looked like she was asleep, her body in a dream state of atonia, though this was a sleep she would never wake from again.

My father called up to me. "Pell! Pell! Come and say goodbye to your mother. Pell, hurry!"

But I was too angry to answer him. I was angry that she hadn't listened to the doctors, angry that she had continued to abuse her body with nicotine, however unreasonable a request that was to make of an addict. I was angry at my father for the salt episode and angry at myself for not interceding, even though I was only a boy at the time. But most of all, I was angry that I hadn't listened to the angels who surely must have tried to warn me while I was listening to Rush.

Now I could hear my sister kissing my mother's forehead, weeping, whimpering.

"Pell! Pell!" my father called up the stairs again. "If you don't come now, you won't be able to say goodbye to her."

I was not going anywhere, though. I sat on the edge of my bed, the door still open, the drumbeats of Neil Peart still hammering away on my headphones. But sometimes, just sometimes, the sound of goodbye is louder than any drumbeat.

I stood up and made my way to the top of the staircase. I couldn't see my mother, only the backs of the paramedics—and my father, who leaned over my mother and whispered her name one last time in her ear.

"Giovanna. Giovanna. Don't leave me. *Please* don't leave me."

And now the tears were streaming down his face and into his mouth, tears of agony and anguish. His tears are of remorse and repentance, sorrow and salt.

And all I can think is, *Enough fucking salt in those tears of yours, Papà?*

CHAPTER 18

The *Janara*

My grandparents' house was old and decrepit, with no insulation and no running water. All our water had to be collected at the public fountain down in the street and then carried up in buckets to the second floor of the house, where all the living quarters were. Washing and bathing was done in large bowls, by hand. The toilet downstairs was an old porcelain bowl perched above a cistern tank—a glorified hole in the ground, basically.

Next door to the toilet was the stable, where my grandfather kept his only mode of transport, a dark gray donkey. The whole of the downstairs area reeked of ammonia, a putrid, pungent concoction of animal and human waste that, when you inhaled, made you feel like you would surely pass out.

Visits to the toilet were usually brief, made all the more hurried by the frequent kicks of the donkey against the thin wall that separated his keratin hoof from my distinctly less solid left ear. That donkey would land his kicks with such power and precision that he made the very foundations of both the house and my brain shudder and jolt.

After a day of baking in the southern Italian sun, that house took as long to cool down at night as a pizzeria oven after a busy Saturday night. All too often, we would wake up sleep-deprived, dazed, and confused.

But every now and then, warm air would rise from the Bay of Naples, skirt around the northern flank of Vesuvius, and gradually make its way upward and eastward toward the leafy mountain slopes of Montevergine, Monteforte, and beyond. On its upward journey, the hot city air would meet the cooler breeze of the Alta Irpinia mountains to form gargantuan towers of fat thunderclouds, which would eventually collapse under their own weight and drench the landscape in cooling late afternoon rain. This was always a welcome reprieve from the fierceness of the July sun and normally meant that you would get at least one good night's sleep.

It was after one of these nights that I remember waking up in the early hours of the morning feeling surprisingly unrested after what should have been a much fresher night than normal. My one thin linen bed sheet lay strewn across the floor beside my bed, a clear indication that I'd been agitated all night. My sense of agitation was accentuated by an unusual heaviness on and in my chest, as if someone had been pressing on it all night.

From the crack in the window shutters, I could see it wasn't quite dawn yet, and I knew my parents would still be asleep. But I couldn't wait anymore, so I made my way into their bedroom.

My mother sat up immediately, got out of her bed, and led me straight out of the room toward the kitchen so as not to wake up my father.

"What is it?" she asks me sleepily.

"I can't sleep. I can't breathe properly, either. And it hurts here," I say, pointing to my sternum.

"You can't breathe?" she inquires. "Are you sick?"

"No, I'm fine," I reply.

My mother then takes me to the kitchen, sits me down at the table, and starts to boil some milk for me. She then opens the window and lets in the predawn air, which is immediately fresh and invigorating.

As she stands over the milk, waiting for it to boil, the only noise that comes out of her mouth is a stifled yawn. Down in the street, we can hear someone sweeping outside their door. The first cockerel crows in the distance, a sign to a pre-alarm clock, pre-internet world that the day is about to begin.

After a couple of minutes, my mother pours the warm milk into a mug, fetches a *biscottino* from the cupboard, and brings it over to me. And then she says the most extraordinary thing.

"It's probably because I forgot to leave a broomstick outside your room."

"A what?"

"A broomstick. If I'd left a broomstick outside your room, you would have slept fine."

"What does a broomstick have to do with me not sleeping well, Mamma?"

"Because then you wouldn't have had a *janara* come visit you last night."

"A what?"

"A *janara*," she repeats, making sure to pronounce it slowly and correctly—*ya-nah-ra*. "A *janara* is a witch. There are lots of them around here."

"Witches, Mamma? Please, don't start! Witches don't exist. And neither do angels, by the way."

"Oh, but they do, *caro mio*. They do. But don't worry. They are not bad witches. They're just sad witches."

My mother then proceeds to tell me all about the Witches of Benevento, or the *janara*, as they call them in the local Irpinia dialect: "After we've all gone to sleep, the *janara* come out of their houses and gather beneath a walnut tree and chant their magic spell."

"Oh, puh-lease, Mamma! Magic spells?"

"Absolutely. Would you like to hear it?"

Without waiting for my answer, she recites the magic spell of the *janara*.

> 'Nguento, 'nguento,
> Mànname a lu nocio 'e Beneviento,
> Sott'a ll'acqua e sotto ô viento,
> Sotto â ogne maletiempo.

"What do the words mean, Mamma?"

"Unguent, unguent, carry me to the walnut tree of Benevento. Above the water and above the wind, and above all other bad weather."

"What's an unguent, Mamma?"

"It's like an ointment. The witches would smear this ointment under their armpits."

"Their armpits? Why?"

"To help them fly!"

I smirk, not even attempting to hide the condescension in my voice at such superstitious nonsense. "I thought witches had broomsticks for that!"

"You're doing it again, Pelli—making fun of me," she replies, frowning at me in a way only a mother can, a timeless blend of disapproval and unconditional love. "I may not have an education like you do, Pelli, but education is much more than just—"

"Reading and writing. Yeah, yeah, I know, Mamma. And in Italian, *educazione* means both 'school' and 'upbringing.' And you're doing it again too. It's Pell, Mamma, not Pelli."

It wasn't until much later on in life, when my mother was no longer *in* my life, that I took the time to properly investigate the concept of witches and flying. My investigation was triggered by a bottle of Strega that caught my eye in a hotel bar in Sorrento. You could hardly miss it, even with so many other bottles of spirits and liqueurs surrounding it, standing tall on the shelf behind the barman, with its distinctive crimson red logo emblazoned across a bright yellow background and, of course, that image of the witches dancing around a walnut tree.

What I discovered on my little search was that witches did indeed apply ointments to their armpits, sometimes their breasts, to help them fly. The ointment in question was made from hallucinogenic plants, such as deadly nightshade and mandrake, both of which are highly psychoactive drugs that produce visions and out-of-body experiences. This small but highly suggestive detail made a deep impression on me and probably explains why years later my fantasy *bruja*, Miss Fifty Shades, would have unusually large sweat patches under her arms.

So, in a way, the witches did fly. At least inside their trippy minds they did. Some witches even applied the ointment to their broom handles, which they then rubbed onto and—more importantly—*into* their vaginas.

Into their vaginas? I didn't believe it at first, not until one of my friends in Spain who was studying art showed me a series of prints by the Spanish artist Francisco Goya called *Los Caprichos*. There were eighty prints, all depicting typically sordid scenes of eighteenth-century Spain, like brothels, salons, and prisons. The prints also delved into themes such as superstition, sensuality, and greed, as well as surreal images from Goya's own dreams and nightmares.

The image this friend wanted to show me was print number 68—*Linda maestra*. There they were, two witches, one young and one old, both very naked, suspended in midair, riding the same broom. The shaft of the broom was nestled so snugly between both women's legs that, had there been any hallucinogenic ointment smeared on it, the effect would have been both immediate and overpowering. There was little doubt that the image had very strong sexual undertones.

Once the witches were fully lubed up with their consciousness-expanding aphrodisiac ointment, they would proceed to run around their walnut tree, broomstick tucked firmly between their loins, and "fly off" to another dimension in some parallel universe, all the while casting their spells on humanity.

Quite a trip *that* must have been! I don't think my mother was aware of that part of the *janara* myth, though.

Then there was the broom itself. These Witches of Benevento used a sorghum broom. A sorghum broom was made with grass or leafy shrubs and is the broom of choice of celebrity witches like the Wicked Witch of the West in the classic film *The Wizard of Oz*.

The other type of broom was a besom broom, which is made from leafless twigs or sprigs. This broom is an altogether darker, blacker, more occult type of broom and is the type Harry Potter and his friends use when they have their first flying lesson at Hogwarts School of Witchcraft and Wizardry.

This distinction is important because it adds another layer to the sexual symbolism of the broomstick of the *janara*—the long, stiff handle being the phallus. The fan-shaped end is the vagina. I can only assume that a *janara* of Benevento would have preferred to have a soft, leafy vagina rather than a brittle, twiggy one.

"So they would put this ointment under their arms and fly off into the night," my mother continues, "often looking for sleeping children."

"Why sleeping children, Mamma?"

"Well, the story I heard was that a *janara* is actually a childless mother, a woman who longs to become a mother but whose wishes have never come true."

Who could have thought as my mother spoke to me in that kitchen that I would one day marry a woman who would experience exactly what it felt like to carry the same void and emptiness as a *janara* of Benevento?

"They like to creep into a child's bedroom at night and watch the child sleeping," my mother continues. "Sometimes they would even lie next to you on the bed, just to feel the warmth of your body while you sleep. Or on top of you."

She lets her last words hang in the air and waits for me to fully grasp the implications of what she just said.

It doesn't take long. My face changes from mild fascination to extreme horror.

"Oh, my God! Are you telling me that's why I couldn't breathe last night? Because a *janara* spent the night on top of me while I was asleep?"

"But they're not bad, Pellegrino. Just sad."

"Fuck sad!" I shriek, as I stand up in horror. "You are freaking me out, Mamma!"

"Watch your language, Pellegrino. I get enough of that kind of language from your father!"

"Sorry, Mamma. Did a *janara* really sleep on top of me last night? Please tell me that's not true!"

"They are not bad, Pell. The *janara* come to warn us, too, if something terrible is about to happen. They are more like angels than witches. They should really be called the *Angels* of Benevento."

"More like the Angels of Hell, Mamma. Hell's Angels."

"Or Pell's Angels," she replies with a wry smile.

We both fall into a heap of laughter, just like we did that time she first told me about angels, and how one particular angel had warned her in an English church in 1961 not to marry my father.

"And remember," she continues, "that *Benevento* means 'good wind'; you know, *bene . . . vento*. The wind that brings good witches. You see, there it is again. 'A vita è bella, pure quanno è brutta. Life is beautiful, even when it's ugly."

"But what has this got to do with leaving a broom outside my room?"

"Well, people say that when you leave a broom outside your room, the *janara* feels compelled to stop and count how many blades of grass the broom has. And since there are so many to count, by the time she is finished, it's almost dawn, she has to get back home, so she never makes it into the room."

"Is that why you have a broom in the kitchen at home, even though you always use a vacuum cleaner?"

"That's right! Lots of houses in Italy have them."

"But yours is not a witch's broom, Mamma. It's a normal modern broom, with hairs."

"Even better!" my mother cries. "Modern brooms have many more hairs than blades of grass on the traditional sorghum brooms. It takes the *janara* even longer to count them. Great for countries with really long winter nights, like Norway. And if you don't have a broom, you can leave a bag of salt instead."

"Salt, Mamma?"

"Yes, salt. Same principle. The *janara* feels the same urge to count grains of salt as she does hairs on a broom. And counting salt takes even longer than counting broom hairs."

"Is that why you didn't put more salt in Papà's sauce, Mamma? To save some for the *janara*, so that they wouldn't sleep on top of me? You did that for me?"

She doesn't answer. Instead, she smiles, strokes me on my cheek, and calmly leaves the room.

CHAPTER 19

A Tsunami of Eye Drops

For years after my mother's death, I stopped believing in a lot of things: God, for a start; angels; and stars—both shooting and lucky. As for believing that a star could actually lead a trio of wise men to some manger where some savior lay in swaddling clothes, well, that was just another example of superstitious crap. I didn't have a story or a myth to explain my mother's death. I needed a destruction myth to rival religion's various creation myths, a tale of a sad witch sitting on my chest, making it hard to breathe. I wished I had an alternative story to tell myself to help explain why she died, to calm my heart and my soul. Any story would do, really—anything other than the story I carried around with me: that my mother brought this on herself, that she did it on purpose.

I mean, she ate too much. She never exercised. She smoked like a chimney—especially the smoking. Her smoking really pissed me off. The doctor had told her to stop smoking—immediately. He'd told her when he was called out to our house because she couldn't move her left arm and the side of her face was all numb. He'd told her again when he referred her to a leading cardiologist in Southampton. That specialist had the same stark message, although I couldn't help thinking at the time that his British understatement and posh grammar-school palaver missed the mark of conveying to my mother the full gravity of her condition.

"You need to lose a few pounds, and you need to rein in your smoking," he told her. What the fuck does that mean? Probably the only words my mother understood were *few* and *smoking*, and that's what she continued to do—smoke a few.

Even when she was rushed to the same hospital in South-ampton a few weeks later, and she was lying there with a saline drip attached to her arm, she still didn't get how close she was to the edge. She still didn't realize that, if she wanted to see her grandchildren, she would need to stop smoking.

I think of that saline drip now and wonder if she actually *did* put less salt in the sauce to help ease her blood pressure. Osmosis may be good as an alternative source of energy, but in the body, fresh blood meeting salty blood is a recipe for elevated blood pressure and unwanted strain on the heart.

But why hadn't she just told my father that, then? Why did she so often choose to stay silent? Why did she put everybody else's needs before hers all the time? Except this one time, when she continued to sneak off to the toilet to smoke. We could all smell it in the house. My father had even told her off a couple of times. But she carried on all the same. Furtively fucking up— and shortening—her own life. She *chose* to leave us, to abandon us—to abandon me. That's the story I have, and it enrages me. How could anyone be so stupid, so irresponsible?

To this day, I still get angry and scared when anyone in my family is sick, even if it's the kids. Something deep in my memory, deep in the core of my soul, is thrown into a state of panic. It's like hitting a panic button, only the button is hypersensitive and linked directly to the automatic trigger of an AK-47. And when that AK-47 fires, it fires blindly and indiscriminately at anything or anyone in its immediate vicinity, spraying its victims with shrieks of "Don't you dare get ill on me now!" and "Get your shit together!" The firing only stops when the last bullet casing has been ejected from the chamber. It's always carnage. Even though I am cognitively aware of the mechanics of my anger, I am emotionally powerless to stop it. And I always feel terrible afterward.

When my mother died, something inside me died with her. For years, I didn't know what it was. I just felt empty. Apart from the actual day that it happened and the day of the funeral, I didn't really cry much at all.

But I started getting drunk a lot, night after night of excessive drinking—and puking. God, did I puke a lot—in the pub toilets, in the *pub* even, in the streets, on the bus on the way home, in the bushes. It was as if I was trying to puke away all my pain.

I didn't enjoy drinking. I never have, really. "For an Italian," people tell me, "you drink an awfully *small* amount of wine." The word *wine*, for me, activates a trigger in my brain that tastes of old socks and paint stripper. All I was after was a readily available anesthetic to numb my pain. Alcohol served that purpose well, at least until the morning.

We didn't talk about my mother's death at home, either. There was no counseling in those days, no real support systems for bereaved children. We had lots of friends and family who did their best to lend a hand, to help with the daily tasks of a normal family, like shopping and the laundry, but as far as having a constructive, healing, soothing conversation about how we felt, we had little or nothing. The only real conversationalist we ever had in our family—at least as far as I was concerned—was my mother, and she was decomposing in a box six feet under the ground.

Besides, I'd been raised to suppress my feelings—at least my weaknesses, my vulnerabilities. I'd been programmed to drown those kinds of feelings, as if they were baby kittens in a sack, tossed into the murky waters of the river Thames.

Among my male cousins in Forino, I'd learned that the right thing to do was chug homemade wine as if it were the nectar of the gods, even throwing in a convincing compliment about its exquisiteness afterward. From my father, I'd learned that if you hated working night shifts, you sucked it up and sulked silently around the house instead of opening up to others about how you found it difficult to manage. When you saw a stray dog, a potential danger to your livestock, you casually pulled out your shotgun, and you fired a piece of lead into its heart. You did it without emotion, without compassion, and *definitely* without crying. I could not allow myself to get too close to my own feelings of vulnerability. I had to conceal them, to protect myself from them—from *others* getting too close to me and seeing me for who I really was: a young, vulnerable man in need of emotional help. And what better way to protect myself than to deploy the weapons that had worked for nearly all the males in my family: anger and violence?

It started with excessive use of force in my school rugby games, stamping and elbowing players from the opposing teams for no reason other than to make them feel some of the pain I was experiencing. I ended up in a lot of fights at school, invariably instigating them and for the most insignificant of reasons. All it took was a comment or joke at my expense, and I would lash out. In the school canteen one day, I punched a fellow student in the face when he said that Italian footballers played like pussies. Then I slammed a chair down on his back as he tried to pull himself back up from the floor. Another time, I brought in my air rifle to school and shot one of my teachers in his buttock. Perhaps the strangest act of violence was an experiment: I cut down a random tree on the school grounds to determine whether removing the oxygen respired by the tree during photosynthesis would cause a human of my choice to die of oxygen starvation. The human I'd chosen for my experiment was Derek. Obviously, it didn't work. I feel dreadfully sorry for that innocent tree—and that boy and even my teacher's backside. Well, maybe not the teacher's backside.

Loss, fear, a sense of abandonment—that's what I felt. I simply didn't have the emotional language—the words, the labels—to describe those emotions. If I lacked the language, at least I could inflict those feelings on others and let them feel what I was feeling. Meanwhile, my anger continued to flourish and fester inside me, poisoning my very being. And like all toxic emotions, anger will always find a way out. That burning coal in the palm of your hand will smolder away, sizzling your skin until you can't bear the pain anymore, until you release it, unleash it, like an Icelandic geyser spewing its sulfuric guts out into the world, spraying everything and everyone with its scorching geothermal plume.

· · ·

"How many eye drops have you taken today?"

I was in a bad mood—again. I was exhausted. Being an international public speaker may sound glamorous, but it's not. It's hotels, airports, taxis, limos, buses, and rental cars—day after day and night after night. Whenever I do make it home to see my family and sleep in my own bed, I usually arrive late at night. I barely have time to say hello and grab some food before I have to head straight down to my office to prepare the next day's talk. This grueling work schedule was brutal when I was a sprightly thirty-year-old; at fifty, it is both excruciating and crucifying. In fact, it is *excrucifying!*

"That's not a feckin' word, Riccardi!" That's what Titch McCarthy would have said. "Plus, it's feckin' superfluous! *Excruciating* and *crucifying* mean the same thing; they both stem from the Latin word *crux*, which means 'cross.' And that is basically the crux of the matter, Riccardi: You can't feckin' have both!"

Well, Titch McCarthy, since my schedule actually does feel like a double crucifixion, I've feckin' decided to officially make it a word now!

I had to be up at five o'clock in the morning to catch the first flight to Frankfurt—or was it Munich? No, wait, that's next week. It's Warsaw tomorrow. My sleep deficit is so bad that it makes the US trade deficit look like a car loan. It was the same thing week after week, month after month, year after year.

While Olivia was asleep last night, I spent fourteen hours on the road, going through security checks, listening to safety announcements. The fast-track queues for the frequent flyers and first-class travelers were full of overtraveled, overweight men who moved so slowly that I mused over whether they should rename the queues "fat tracks" instead.

So I take naps on the sofa on the weekends—horrible, unsatisfying naps. They are little more than vain attempts to reset my circadian rhythms, but I never sleep well during these naps. I never feel rested when I wake up again. Who would? The human body isn't designed to sleep in spurts, during the day, on the couch. The expression in English is "to get a good night's sleep," not "to get a good *day's* sleep."

All the traveling takes its toll, wears me down, pisses me off. It makes me focus on the insignificant microdetails of my life and turn them into macroanalogies of everything that's wrong with the world. Everything seemed so much easier before I started a family, before I became an immigrant in Norway, the country that my wife had *explicitly* promised would make me happy.

I really want to work less—fewer hours, less travel—but ever since Olivia came along, life had become even more expensive. Suddenly, the house we lived in was too small, so we moved into a new one, along with a new mortgage. A friend in Spain had quipped, "Well that's just delayed your retirement by about ten years." He was right. It had. Olivia was now a contender for being Norway's most expensive baby, both in monetary terms and psychological ones.

But she was worth it. All of my children are worth it; of course they are. But especially Olivia. Olivia was the reason I knew that my wife and I were right for each other. She is how I knew for sure that my plumbing worked properly, that I functioned properly, as a real man should.

So, like a real man, I bite the bullet and get on with making a living, providing for my family, feeling useful. I am a man on a mission. I rack up those air miles, channel those earnings into the now-deferred retirement fund and the rainy-day account that my father never had, so that, at least, if I should die of exhaustion along the way, my family will be taken care of.

However, no amount of money will fool the biological rhythms of the body into believing that irregular sleeping patterns are good for it, especially sleeping during the day.

Now I'm up again after my nap, my forehead throbbing from today's unsatisfactory sleep and from years of intermittent sleep deprivation. My hair is still wet from the shower I have just taken to help wake me up, to help remove the grime of hotels, airports, taxis, limos, buses, and rental cars. The smell of shampoo wafts across the living room and into the kitchen, competing with the savory odors of cheap oregano, fake tomato sauce, and second-rate Parmesan from the pasta my wife has made for dinner.

I am in a bad mood again, and I turn to my wife and ask her again, "How many eye drops did you take today?"

. . .

Meibomian gland dysfunction—that's the name of the disease she'd contracted not long after Olivia was born. MGD means that the glands in the eyelids have stopped producing the all-important oil called meibum that lubricates the eyes. Meibum stops your tears from evaporating too quickly. An eye without meibum oil is like a combustion engine without oil.

Like many diseases, you can get a mild form of MGD, or you can get a serious one. On a scale of one to ten, where ten is the most serious, my wife's is Spinal Tap: It's an eleven! It's an up-at-dawn siege of excruciating pain that doesn't stop until she falls asleep again. On a bad day, even something as mundane as blinking can become an agonizing operation. It's like having a piece of sandpaper stitched to the inside of her eyelid. If you stop to consider that, on average, we blink 9,600 times a day, then you can begin to appreciate what kind of pain she goes through.

Who knows how long she'd had the disease before she actually went to a doctor to get some treatment. As ever, she was silent, stoic, and serene in her suffering, just like when she was trying to get pregnant with Olivia's brother and sister all those years ago. She sat through the blood tests, Pap smear tests, urine tests, hormone tests, and needles to inject the drugs that would cheat her uterus into producing a score of eggs, and not once did she complain then, so it would take a lot more now. It would appear that I am not alone in drowning my emotions quietly.

I tried to help. I tried to fix it, just like Luigi would have done—our good old hillbilly Mr. Fixit. Or like the good ol' doctor at the Andrology Centre did when he untwisted my epididymis. Or like the blue diamonds to help fix my ED. Because that's what men like to do, right? We fix things. We fix problems; we fix people. And in the end, after everything else in the world has been fixed—and not before—we fix ourselves.

The clinics in Norway had been fruitless, futile, and hopeless. The main problem was how to relieve her chronic pain. They couldn't prescribe her opioids because one of their main side effects was xerostomia—the drying up of the mouth, as well as practically any part of the body that had moisture in it, including the eyes. The pain was so bad that she even considered having her eyes surgically removed. She'd read about it on an MGD forum that some patients found the condition so unbearable that they opted for blindness rather than to endure everlasting, agonizing pain. Evidently, plenty of blind people had rich and fulfilling lives, something that could not be said for people with MGD chronic pain.

I had pleaded to the Norwegian eye doctor for some help.

"Look, there must be something we can do for the pain. My wife is desperate. She's suicidal."

"There's very little we can do, I'm afraid. Have you considered a pain management clinic?" the doctor replied laconically.

"Doctor, I've read about a clinic in London that specializes in this disease, and they say they use a designer steroid called Lotemax to combat the pain."

The doctor's body language changed instantly. He seemed annoyed. Affronted.

"I strongly advise you not to use that. It can cause irreparable damage to the eyes. That's why we don't supply it here in Norway."

"But it's been tested in the UK with very encouraging results," I told the doctor. "It's worth a shot, surely."

A few weeks later, we were in a Harley Street clinic in London. *Those air miles and those extra earnings are coming in handy now*, I think. They were paying for some of the best and most pioneering medical work in the world. And they were paying for those lifesaving eye drops.

There is hope, I reassure myself. My wife, though, finds it much harder to muster up the same level of hope. She remains forlorn and hopeless. She just can't get those two words that the doctor used out of her head: "irreparable damage."

I wish the eye doctor could have said what the IVF doctor had said: "Sooner or later, one way or another, the vast majority of women who want to get relief for their chronic pain do get relief. And they get it from a magic eye drop called Lotemax." But he wouldn't do that. He wouldn't commit himself to something he couldn't guarantee, not even hope. Instead, that was my job, which is why I need to make sure my wife keeps taking her drops, because they work. They are the only topical medication that helps her with her chronic pain.

That's why I am asking her how many eye drops she has taken today. Because she isn't taking them. She hasn't taken any. She isn't going to, not if it is going to cause "irreparable damage." She sees no hope.

She pretends to not hear me.

"I said, how many fucking eye drops did you take today?"

I do my best to stay calm, but I'm already struggling. I know that the eye drops work. I saw that in the evanescent smile that spread across my wife's face the first time she took them.

I also know—because the eye doctor told us so—that, as long as we monitor the pressure in her eyeball, she will be fine. Elevated pressure in her eye will be a problem. The doctor did not sugarcoat anything. There was no hint of British understatement in his warning. If the pressure rises, stop the eye drops, or risk consequences that *will* be irreparable. She'd had several checks by now, with no signs of even so much as an iota of difference in pressure. Zero. Nada. Zilch. No need to start looking for a surgeon to remove her eyes, then.

"So? How many?"

"One dose this morning," she replies.

"Are you sure? You don't look like you've taken one this morning."

She tries to force a smile, but the unmistakable furrows on her brow tell me she is suffering today. After so many years with her, I can read her like a Ladybird book, her every micro expression. I know she hasn't taken the fucking drops.

All I want is to fix her. Fucking fix her. All I want is to be useful, to be admired for my ability to solve her problems—to save her, perhaps. But she is no driveway full of snow that I can just apply brute force to. I don't care that all she wants right now is some comfort, some empathy, and some compassion. All I care about is fixing her. But she has to *want* to be fixed.

The sense of inadequacy that fills me now further stokes the frustration and anger. And all of a sudden, the most appalling, most repellent thought enters my mind: She is doing this on purpose. She knows what is good for her, but she does the opposite—just like my mother did in the weeks and months leading up to that rainy Monday morning in October when I was trying to learn Neil Peart's drum parts.

Yes, that's it! It's *her actions* that are making me feel inadequate. That deep abyss of inadequacy has never completely left me. It was always there, like a pilot light on a gas fire. However much my wife tried to extinguish that flame, that pilot light of rage kept on quivering away in my very soul. All it took was the tiniest of sparks to turn that pilot light into an inferno. Today, it looks like that the spark will be eye drops.

My mirror neurons have been switched off by the rage that has started to well up inside of me. The rage is fueled by the belief that my wife is doing this on purpose, as a self-destructive act of spite. She is sabotaging her own road to recovery by going against the advice of her doctor—her English doctor, that is. She *has* to listen to the English doctor. She *has* to stop smoking in secret in the bathroom. . . . No, wait. That's a different mother. . . . She *has* to stop pretending to take the drops.

"But they are so expensive, and we can't keep going to London for treatment," she argues. "It's not fair on you. You already work so hard for us all."

"I'll be the judge of that. Just take your fucking drops."

No matter how hard I work, no matter how many five o'clock flights and ineffective afternoon naps, I can always afford to take a trip to London with my wife, right? What is the point of earning all those air miles and money if I can't put it all to good use? And I could certainly afford to buy a pack of fucking eye drops, with fancy wrapping and all, if necessary.

So we sit around the table, three steaming plates of pasta in front of us: one for each of my girls and one for me. Christian is at football practice. Just one plate is missing—my wife's. She is still dishing out her own plate. She always serves herself last.

While she is still at the stove, I tuck in, shoveling a heaping mound of spaghetti into my mouth. Then I drop my fork noisily onto the plate.

"Did you hear me, woman? I asked how much fucking salt you put in the sauce!"

"What? Did you just call me 'woman'? What salt? What are you talking about?"

"I mean. . . . No, not the salt. . . . I asked you how many fucking drops you took today."

It would have been much more constructive if I had just said what was on my mind without the verbal assault on the woman I loved. But I hadn't learned how to do that. Nobody had taught me how to show vulnerability, fear. The ultimate nightmare, of course, was losing another mother—the mother of my children.

Instead, I was about to pass the point of no return, the point at which I provoke a response from my wife—the mother of my children—and therefore justify retaliation and eventual escalation.

Aggression displacement, they call it. Apparently, it works too. It makes the aggressor feel better, if only for a brief moment.

Mother ignores the provocation. She takes her plate of pasta and sits down at the table.

"But the doctor in Norway said that it could cause irreparable damage."

"Another twat who knows fuck all about fuck all!"

My swear rate has gone up; two fucks and a twat in a nine-word sentence—a ratio of three to one. That is not good. That line of logic would certainly not have been approved of in my Balloon Debate Sessions at St. Brendan's, not even if I'd managed to say it in Latin.

What's about to happen now is inevitable, irreversible. We all knew what was coming. We'd seen it before: a Pellegrino Riccardi rant. It would be a rant of biblical proportions, the kind Quentin Tarantino would have been proud of.

"Why the fuck do I bother living in this fucking country? The doctors are so far up their own holier-than-thou, conservative arses that they can't see or learn what's going on in the medical profession. You can't even get a Strepsil or a Lemsip without a fucking prescription in this fucking backwater hillbilly farmer mentality shithole of a country! What the hell did I move to this fucking country for? Why in the Pope's name do I bother going to work? To come home to a bunch of ignorant twats who know fuck all about fuck all? Why the—"

But before I can finish my Tarantinian monologue, my wife cuts me down with fateful words. "Oh, leave me the fuck alone! If you find me dead one morning on the kitchen floor, then know that I killed myself for two reasons: to stop this pain and to stop having to listen to your bullshit!"

Every time I visualize what happened next, it happens in slow motion, even though, in reality, it couldn't have taken more than twenty seconds—thirty, max.

I slam my hand down on the table, so hard that it probably changes the direction of the grain in the wood. I feel the pain and the heat searing through my palms and up to my brain—not as hot as when Om grasped the glowing tap in chemistry class, but certainly as hot, if not hotter, than when Derek strafed my palms that evening after school. In one smooth movement, my right arm rises above my head, and I launch it up and down around the scruff of my wife's neck. Sixty to nought in point one of a second. Instant and total transfer of energy from my hand to her body.

She lets out a scream—a silent scream, like a lamb about to be slaughtered for the feast. Now she's moving. No, she's being dragged like a plow through a field of sodden clay, silently, her wide, terrified eyes begging her daughters to help.

They can read her eyes, but they can't move. They are stuck to their chairs. Flight, fight, or freeze. They freeze like cherub statues. *Cui bono?* Titch McCarthy. *Cui bono?* What good is it for? That's what they would be saying if they could speak Latin. They watch as their mother is dragged past them toward the kitchen, still screaming silently. How can you scream without making a noise? You do it with your eyes, with the whites of your eyes.

And now we are both in the kitchen, my hand still clenched around the scruff of her neck. I pull open the cutlery drawer and frantically scour the inside for something. Now I have a knife in my hand—a fucking knife! Like a lamb to slaughter.

Pappa, no. Pappa, no.

And all I can say to her as she looks at me with no love in her eyes is, "Are you sure you took your eye drops?"

Here I am, surrounded by my angels—Pell's angels—an alpha male who has successfully displaced his aggression onto what he treasures most, the most important people, the most significant relationships in his life, the most important *women* in his life.

My angels are looking at me in all my pathetic tragedy. I am at the lowest point in my life. I am in the ninth circle of hell, in the deepest recess of hell, along with Lucifer, Brutus, Cassius, and Judas. We are all men who are guilty of the same crime as I am: treachery, betrayal, and infidelity.

The distance between my wife and me cannot be any larger. The mid-Atlantic Ridge that had been forming between us, imperceptible for so many years, is now undeniable. We are like two tectonic plates that have finally collapsed under their own weight of discontent and alienation. I am the earthquake that destroys cities and calls forth tsunamis. And I am drowning in my own tsunami of shame and self-loathing.

Olivia looks at her mother. Her Teletubby vocabulary is unable to express the emotions in her heart, but I can swear that the whites of her eyes are saying one thing: "Oh, Mamma. Please tell me that life is beautiful even when it's ugly."

CHAPTER 20

A Woman's Eyes and a Hillbilly's Hands

I do not want to divulge the minutiae of what we all went through as a family in the months that followed that violent episode. You can imagine for yourself how difficult it was, for *all* of us. I am not going to try to excuse or justify what I did. I am not going to defend it. I am not going to blame anyone but myself. Neither am I looking for pity or forgiveness from you, the reader. You can hate me, despise me, or pity me. That's your right, your prerogative. You decide.

What I will tell you is that, whatever you do think about me, I have probably already thought the same thoughts about myself. What I can also tell you is that during the weeks and months that followed, our home was Olivia's drawing: a house with crooked windows and lopsided chimneys that looked like it would topple off at any moment. I have never found out if that drawing was Olivia's way of communicating her anxiety and pain to us, a way of compensating for her limited and ultimately inadequate Teletubby vocabulary. All I did was get angry at her.

But I wasn't angry at *her*. I was angry at me, for allowing myself to let it go so far, to the point where I had exploded. I detested the person that I had shown myself to be, if only for an exceptional, uncharacteristic moment. A man's only escape from his old self is to see a different self mirrored in a woman's eyes. That day in the kitchen, I saw a self that I had not seen before and that I never want to see again. And I saw it through the eyes of the most important women in my life: my wife and my two daughters—my angels.

The reflection that I saw horrified and disgusted me. I was filled with a sense of shame and remorse that I sometimes struggle to deal with even today. That feeling of shame was not diminished in any way when two women from the Norwegian Child Protection Services made their procedural call to our house to observe the interaction between me and my children. My wife had talked about the episode with her psychologist, something that had obligated her to override doctor-patient privilege and inform the authorities.

This is something I fully support. It should be like this.

The NCPS women wanted to make sure that my kids were comfortable around me, that they warmed to me as a child should to a caring, loving parent. They wanted to ensure that I was a father to them and not a source of fear and violence.

It was a short visit, with no subsequent action or repercussions. I guess they picked up pretty quickly on the positive vibe between my children and me. They could see that I was essentially a good father, that my kids were not afraid of me, and that I posed little or no threat to my family. What had happened had been a one-off. It'd had the potential to be a much more calamitous one-off, but the reality of it all was that it hadn't turned out that way.

The NCPS left, satisfied that I was not a future threat to my family. Because I am not.

Neither was my shame lessened when I was interviewed by another woman, this time at the organization Alternative to Violence in Oslo, another procedural obligation of the System. Her job was to assess my psychological condition and risk of further violent acts toward my family. This too was a short interview. She wrote her report, which I still have at home, and we never saw each other again.

I guess she too was satisfied that I was not a future threat to my family. Because I am not.

So, why did I retell one of the most shameful and horrific episodes in my life? Why did I choose to tell you, the reader, about a violent—albeit one-off—shameful event? Simply because shame feeds on secrecy. The longer you keep your shame a secret, the longer its flames will scorch your soul. By removing the secrecy, you can begin to deal with and heal from your shame. By showing your vulnerability, by being brave enough to expose your pain points and weaknesses to others, you are more likely to receive love and support from those who care about you.

This applies particularly to men. My appeal to men is to talk to others about your pain. Expose your weaknesses, your short-comings, your vulnerabilities. Rip open your shirt and expose your breastplate. Tear off the armor. Hell, even shave your beards and let other men see your micro expressions of fear, uncertainty, and pain.

It will hurt at first, but the hurt will eventually subside as you allow others into your vulnerable world. Remember that the shields we men put up to protect our vulnerabilities—in my case, mostly anger and silence—only serve to keep people at a distance. They communicate to others that they should stay away. So they do. And we men remain as lonely and in pain as before, if not more.

Men! Put down your shields. Lay aside your misguided protection and displaced aggression. Tell others that you are hurting, that you need them. More often than not, your true friends and family will respond warmly to your gesture and give you exactly what you are looking for. Not only will they help you, but they will respect you and love you even more. They may even admire you for it.

But most of all, do it before you end up exploding like I did. Do it before the frustration, anger, and self-loathing builds up to a level where you can't hold it back anymore and you end up doing something you regret for the rest of your life.

After all, men, deep down inside, we are just like children. We think we know what we want but have no idea what we need. And what we need is to open up to others about our fears.

. . .

"You know you can lie down on the sunbed, Luigi?"

"I know. I know," replies Luigi, and promptly flips himself over onto his stomach so that he can carry on soaking in the sun's rays on the limestone parapet that surrounds the swimming pool. In true Luigi style, he has opted for the rough texture of stone on his body to the softer, more conventional materials of a sunbed or a deck chair. As he lies there on his masonry bed, facedown, I can almost hear his red neck and broad shoulders begin to sizzle like pancetta in a pan.

"Doesn't that hurt," I ask him, "lying on those sharp stones?"

"Pain is good, Pellegrino," he replies in his usual deadpan manner. "Without a bit of pain, you can't appreciate pleasure. Even Jesus suffered, Pellegrino. Even Jesus suffered."

"So, what you're saying is that suffering is good?"

"I didn't say suffering is good, like I *enjoy* suffering, but sometimes it's necessary," Luigi explains, as if he were a priest talking to his congregation. "And besides, it keeps me grateful. And it keeps me sharp. Alert."

"The wall?"

"The suffering," replies Luigi, clearly growing impatient at my skeptical, "educated" probing of his point of view.

He then lets out a somewhat labored groan and nestles his powerful torso into the jagged contours of the stone.

"Ah, this is the life!" he murmurs.

Olivia looks up from her toys and points at Luigi. "Uncle Luigi sleeping, Pappa."

"Soon, Olivia, soon. If we keep quiet, maybe he'll fall asleep."

"Shhh," Olivia says as she places her petite finger on her lips. "Auntie Rosa sleeping too, Pappa."

"No, Auntie Rosa is still awake," my sister pipes up from her comfortable sunbed. Her suntan is coming along nicely. She loves to sizzle in the midday sun. Another rasher of pancetta, just like her husband, the only difference being that my sister's pancetta skin has a bit of English bacon in it, so she sizzles a little faster than Luigi.

The heat of the southern Italian sun is intensifying. I adjust the parasol for Olivia and reposition her sunhat on her head. The thick sheen of factor 50+ sun cream on her body gives her an anemic ghost appearance. *A small price to pay*, I think. *She could have been a daughter of Vincenzo Riccardi in the 1970s.*

Olivia's brother and sister are inside on their iPads. Behind the thick, cool walls of the trullo, they are safe from the pounding of the sun. Meanwhile, my wife has started preparing lunch, her introvert Nordic persona grateful that she has a valid excuse to leave her guests while she too finds respite from the torridness outside.

And it's quiet—dead quiet. Were it not for the crickets in the surrounding olive groves and the occasional sloshing of the water against the underside of the pool's ledge, there would be complete silence now.

I am sitting in the shade of an ancient Apulian olive tree. That old tree has stood there for hundreds of years. Who knows how many times it has seen the trullo dismantled and rebuilt every time the tax collectors paid a visit? Who knows how many generations have worked and lived on the property? How many people have lived and died here? Who knows how deep its roots go into the soil, reaching far beyond the stone wall confines of the garden that it stands in now?

I wonder why the people who converted the trullo decided to spare *that* particular tree from the woodcutter's saw. Sure, they'd wanted to keep a solitary symbolic reminder of what the property used to look like before middle class families like ours began spending their holidays here, but why that particular one? Had they felt sorry for it as it feebly reached down toward the pool's edge like an old man trying to do up his laces? Would they have let that olive tree live if they'd known that Mother Nature and destiny would conspire to allow a child named Olivia to pass below an olive branch and offer her no hope?

. . .

Hillary Clinton called food "the oldest diplomatic tool" in relationship building.[1] Before the final signing of the US-Iran nuclear deal in 2015, the two countries spent twenty arduous months negotiating the deal in a climate of extreme tension and distrust. The talks came precariously close to collapsing on more than one occasion.

Of those twenty months negotiating, nineteen and a half of them were spent eating their meals in separate rooms. That all changed on July 4, 2015, when the Iranians extended an invitation to the Americans on their Independence Day to break bread together. The only condition they requested was that nobody talk shop over the meal. Within ten days of that first meal together, they signed the deal. Experts on both sides were convinced that the meal was the main catalyst for consolidation and agreement.

---

1 Soraya Auer, "Diplomacy on the Menu: How Food Can Shape Politics," *BBC News*, April 26, 2018, https://www.bbc.com/news/world-asia-43901821.

Food can be a peacemaker, a unifier. Food can also be a comforter, a soothing balm for the pain you've had to go through, as well as the pain you know you will have to endure. What was one of the last things Jesus did before he was crucified? He shared a meal with his closest friends. He broke bread with his brothers.

Even prisoners on death row are allowed a final culinary request before their execution, no matter how heinous their crime. I don't know why, but I find great solace in that gesture—a sense of hope and optimism for humanity, even though the context within which this token kindness is framed in is something I abhor.

Most of the prisoners opt for a final carb-and-cholesterol binge. It's not as if you have to worry about dying of a heart attack anymore, is it? Although it *would* also be an ironic final "fuck you" to the executioners to die before they inject their lethal potion into you.

Convicted murderer Victor Feguer requested what must be history's most minimalist and symbolic last supper. He asked for a single unpitted olive, saying that he hoped that the tree that symbolizes peace and hope would sprout from his grave. The pit of the olive was found in Feguer's suit when they buried him. I think I would like to be buried with an olive in my pocket too.

Inviting someone to join you for a meal sends an important message of reconciliation, of union. It keeps that old idealistic belief alive that there is humanity in everyone. Remember, even Nazis loved their children.

So, when I left my three-year-old alone by the pool and headed for the kitchen, it wasn't *only* because of the alluring smell of sizzling garlic in a pan of olive oil. It wasn't *only* because those San Marzano tomatoes smelled so fresh and enticing. It wasn't *only* because I wanted to help out. I was on a mission of peace, seeking reconciliation with the woman that I had aggressed and violated. Food was going to help me do that, because food humanizes people.

Most importantly, food humanizes your adversary, your rival, and your attacker. In the years leading up until that moment, I had ever so slowly but ever so surely become my wife's adversary too, her attacker, her violator. At least, that's what I saw when I looked into the mirror of her eyes. And the shame of it was killing me. I needed to escape from my shame. I needed to escape from my old self—to see a different self in the mirror of my woman's eyes.

I loved my wife. I believed she still had it in her to love me too. At the very least, I was her children's father, and surely it must take a lot to unlove the father of your children, right? I wanted my wife to see the humanity in me again. I wanted to win back her affection, her warmth, her tenderness. I wanted her to see not only the father of her children in me, but the person she fell in love with in the first place.

· · ·

I can feel it again. It's the same quivering reverberation up my spine, the same humming in my veins, the same ghostly eeriness the last time the angels whispered to me. But I am not listening—again.

I am too focused on reconnecting with my wife. We've been through too much to lose it now. Fuck, I have been through too much to let our life together slip away: IVF, rectal examinations, masturbatoriums and Hungarian porn, epididymis realignment, Viagra—really *excrucifying* Viagra. I've stepped up when my wife has hissed "It's time" in my ear, even though I am not a hyena. I've choked on antisnoring gumshields and a tonsillectomy and struggled through a month of lisping because of my new front teeth.

But the rage, the violence—it has always been there, lurking in the shadows of my upbringing. My *educazione*. Titch, Ninuccio, Derek—the cunt—and my father. So much violence. Worst of all was the violence toward my mother. And all because of some salt? No wonder my mother asked my father when he was going to die. But *she* died first.

I should have been listening to the angels that morning too. Instead, I'd been listening to Rush. Learning the drumbeats. But isn't a goodbye supposed to be so much louder than any drumbeat? And now Mr. Peart has left us too, banging away on his drum riser in the sky, hopefully explaining to my mother why it was so important for me to learn all his licks.

But why do these angels have to whisper? Just shout, for fuck's sake! I don't want to lose another person dear to me. I don't want to lose another mother. My wife is the most important mother in my life, more important than my own mother. *Definitely* more important than Mother Nature. Fuck Mother Nature!

I call out to my wife from the pool.

"Trine! Trine, let me give you a hand there in the kitchen!"

She can't hear me, of course, not through those thick limestone trullo walls. But I just need to call out her name.

Because, yes, my wife does have a name. I just couldn't bring myself to use it before now in the book, at least not before I'd put the shame of what I'd done to her in the kitchen behind me. She was too far away from me, emotionally. Even after all the shit we'd been through together, I was fading from her memory, because I was her aggressor, her violator, her adversary.

But now I want her back. I need to go to her. I need to call her name.

"Trine!"

A man has only one escape from his old self: to see a different self in the mirror of some woman's eyes. And so I stand up and make my way toward the kitchen. Toward my mirror.

· · ·

Two small arms reach above the silky waterline, slicing gently through the surface like twin fleshy periscopes. Two arctic blue eyes strain to focus through the blurry chlorine water on the image at the bottom of the pool. A drooping branch of the ancient olive tree feebly reaches down toward her like an old man trying to do up his laces. Below the waterline, the two tiny lungs will soon need air. Those lungs are no bigger than the birthday balloons her father hung up for her on the beams of the poolside pergola only the day before, and they are starting to burn like the candles on her cake. Like any three-year-old, she has no idea what she needs, only what she wants, and what she wants right now is to find out what that drawing at the bottom of the pool is.

And the angels start to whisper, while my bones begin to quiver and my veins begin to hum. But I am not listening.

I don't know how to listen. I am too cocky, too self-absorbed. Too "educated"—even though, as my mother told me, *educazione* means both school and upbringing, "and you, my boy, are not finished with either one yet." I am too wrapped up in my own fantasies of how I want things to be instead of listening to how things actually are.

But Luigi is listening. *He* can feel it, the humming in his veins, the whispering in his ears. He can feel it oscillating through the limestone wall pressing hard against his chest as his back sizzles away like pancetta. He can feel it because he has always been anchored to his Irpinian culture. He has always been rooted to his Forino heritage, in touch and in harmony with his redneck hillbilly Irpinian legacy, a legacy where tripped-out witches roam the villages at night and women stuff scissors down their bras on their wedding days. My Catholic, theocentric, scientific-realist "education" taught me to look down on things like superstition. But just the fact that people like Luigi are willing to buy into superstitions says so much about their willingness to be receptive to the mysteries we simply can't explain with science—like angels.

Luigi can feel it because he comes from a place where home-made wines are shamelessly flaunted alongside their fancy-labeled DOCG counterparts, where authenticity wins over façade, always. Even if authenticity does taste like old socks dipped in paint stripper.

He is connected. He listens. He senses. Right now, he senses the uneven surface of the top of the wall digging into his hip bone and into his toenails. It hurts. But pain is good. It keeps him grateful. It keeps him sharp. It keeps him alert.

Sleep beckons him. Sleep tempts him. Sleep lures him. The gentle rippling of water against the pool's edge and the persistent chirping of crickets in the olive groves around him mesmerize him, anesthetize him. "Fall into my arms," sleep whispers into his ears. "It's time," she hisses.

His eyelids flicker as his brain prepares to go offline, as Olivia passes below the overhanging branch of the olive tree, the one tree that was not cut down. It is a solitary symbolic reminder—but of what? Of death?

If only that ancient olive could reach down and take her hand, lift her to safety. If only that branch were as young and supple as that child. Then it could stretch a little farther, all the way down to the glistening waterline. Then it could hold out a small olive leaf of hope for Olivia to grab onto.

The angels continue to whisper, but he thinks the angels are just part of some trippy dream he's having where words are uttered out of context and images become a collage of impressions.

He releases another labored groan as he nestles his powerful torso into the jagged contours of the stone and turns his head toward the house, toward the pool.

He sees two small arms reaching above the silky waterline, slicing gently through the surface like twin fleshy periscopes. He sees her smooth fingers sticking out from the water like feeble anemones swaying aimlessly in the current, without any visible sign of concern or agitation. Why should a child feel agitated when she knows that her father is close at hand to keep her safe?

But where is he?

And the angels are still whispering in his ear—louder now. Or perhaps it's the silence that is louder, so deafening that it has muted the persistent chirping of crickets.

Every time Luigi visualizes what happens next, it happens in slow motion, even though, in reality, it couldn't have taken more than twenty seconds—thirty, max.

He leaps up from the wall like a surfer mounting his board. The sudden rush of blood to his head sends him spinning. He can feel a painful tingling on his chest. Only later, once the adrenaline has subsided, will he work out that some of the hairs on his chest were ripped out when they snagged on the jagged edges of the stone wall.

He steadies himself, sees the fingers sinking lower, lower into the water. And then he runs. He runs toward the fingers, toward those tiny lungs that surely cannot hold on any longer. But she is on the far side of the pool. He has to jump in.

His legs have no idea where the stony edge of the pool ends and where the water begins. He may even have walked on the water's surface for a couple of strides, such was the agility and speed with which he moved toward his niece. He only knows that the splash of the water sizzles on his sun-parched skin and in the empty follicles of his chest hair.

As he wades desperately toward Olivia, he reaches out his

hands, his huge, callous-ridden hands. Those hands have powerful, vice-like fingers that have clasped at and lifted countless blocks of granite and limestone with the ease of an industrial crane. Those fingers have biceps. And he thrusts them into the water, grabs Olivia, and launches her out of the water.

Olivia's eyes are open. But they are blank. The whites of her eyes—the scleras—are larger than normal, but they communicate nothing. There is no fear, no anxiety, nothing. And that's the problem. Just when you need her scleras to communicate something, to reveal her inner needs and emotions, they say nothing. She knows what she wants, and she knows what she needs, too: air.

Her body is limp, and her chest is motionless. Luigi scrambles up the small steps of the pool. He then lifts her up with one arm and starts to bang her back with the other—instinctively, vigorously, aggressively, lovingly.

The last time he'd held her over water was at her baptism, when he stood as godfather to her. He'd held her lovingly there, too. "I baptize you in the name of the Father, the Son, and the Holy Spirit." Luigi had vowed to come to her aid if ever her father could not. That is, after all, what an Italian godfather's role is.

Her lips are blue. Her eyes are glazing over. Her body is cold, wet, and lifeless—as lifeless as those many other children on Utøya that day in July, when Olivia was just a few days old. That was another day when men failed to protect a child, a son, a daughter.

The angels have ceased their whispering. The olive trees have stopped shimmering in the afternoon breeze. Even the crickets have muted their normally incessant chirping, almost as if it were a mark of respect. Mother Nature takes a deep breath, and the silence is somber and majestic as Luigi holds Olivia in his masculine arms.

Suddenly, the silence is broken by the splatter of water on the limestone tiles. Warm, chlorine water splashes onto Luigi's feet. And then he hears the whisper of a deep, deep breath. That breath is smaller than Mother Nature's but just as vital, just as life-giving. It is followed by a scream—first in pain and then in relief and confusion.

Luigi turns Olivia the right way up again and gazes into her eyes, straight into those arctic blue eyes. They are awash with salty tears, streaming down her face. She is afraid but not alone. Her godfather bursts into tears too—fearful, grateful tears.

He holds her to his chest, grasping her with his huge hands, encircling her in his mighty arms. Those same huge arms built his home, made his own wine, reached out to shake my hand when he asked if he could date my sister. Those are lifesaving hands.

Life *is* beautiful, even when it's ugly.

Epilogue

I often wonder what my life would have been like if Luigi hadn't heard those angels whispering in his ear. I wonder whether the shared tragedy of losing a child would have brought me and Trine closer together or pushed us further apart. Many couples who lose a child do indeed end up leaving each other. There are studies that claim that as many as 80 percent end up in divorce, while other studies suggest that the figure is around 16 percent. What I find to be more relevant and interesting are the reasons why couples who *do* decide to go their separate ways do so. There are four key factors that affect whether a couple survives a bereavement or not.

Factor 1: How Strong the Relationship Was before the Loss

In our case, seriously jeopardized. In the opening chapter, I wrote that we "had been drifting from one another for some time, like sailboats on a Sargasso Sea of ennui and weariness." Olivia was certainly the long-awaited wind that filled our sails again, and for a while at least, we sailed happily alongside each other. However, it wasn't long before our boats started heading in different directions.

Much of the blame for that drifting apart falls on me, insomuch as I was unwilling or unable to express my feelings and emotions, especially those that centered on my shortcomings and vulner-abilities. Instead, I chose to suppress and disguise those feelings, opting to drown quietly in the shame of my sense of inadequacy, surfacing only to blow off steam with my Icelandic-geyser rants and rages. One of those eruptions happened in my kitchen, and its sheer force and brutality sent us hurtling on paths of separation.

Factor 2: The Cause and Circumstances Surrounding the Loss

In our case, my fault and my fault alone. That day by the pool, I—and I alone—was responsible for Olivia's safety. Instead of *assuming* that my sister and Luigi were watching over Olivia, I should have checked and double-checked that they had taken over my duties. I know this. Trine knows this. Had events panned out for the worse, I would have never been able to forgive myself. More importantly, though, I suspect that *Trine* would never have been able to forgive me.

Factor 3: The Coping Skills Each Person Had before the Loss

In our case, not many, and the ones I did have didn't work very well. Prior to that summer's day in Italy, I used to think that showing "softer" emotions was unbecoming of a man. I could display anger—that was okay—but not vulnerability or uncertainty or weakness, all of which deserved to be buried deep inside my LinkedIn/Facebook persona and concealed from public view. If I were to be a guest on Dr. Phil, he would probably have asked me, "How's that working for you?," to which I would have had no other answer than, "It's not!"

My strategy of manning up ended up creating an almost bottomless pit of shame inside me, something I kept secret. And shame loves secrecy. Shame feeds on it. Secrecy is the rocket fuel of shame. This is why I have written this book. Not because I want your sympathy or your pity but because by exposing my shame, I am starving it of its major source of fuel.

Factor 4: How Much Support the Couple Gets

In our case, questionable; in my case, probably not that much. If I hadn't written this book, I am pretty sure that I would have handled the situation in the same emotionally incompetent way as I'd always done. This would have involved keeping both my "weaker" and "softer" emotions at bay while at the same time sending out false signals to my immediate circle of friends and family that I didn't need their help—that I was fine, when, in actual fact, I was *far* from fine. In other words, I would have ended up getting little or no support.

So, based on these four key factors, I can only conclude that Trine and I would have split up. But we didn't. Today, we are still together, dealing with everything life has to offer—and throw at us—as best we can. After the initial aftershock and post-traumatic numbness we felt at so nearly losing our youngest child, we found ourselves clinging on to the same mutual feelings of gratitude and humility at our good fortune.

I am convinced that the incident in Italy on that hot summer's day kept us together, *for better and for worse*. I also know that when I look into Trine's eyes, I see a different self than the man I used to see. I can absolutely live with that.

In the years that have passed, there have been no more "kitchen incidents"—not even nearly. At the same time, I know I was lucky—*really* lucky—that I didn't end up doing something much worse, something that I would have regretted even more than I do now. This is why I urge men to speak out about their shortcomings, inadequacies, and fears. Starve your shame of its fuel—secrecy.

My message to you is simple: It's okay to not be okay. And if you happen to be the person on the receiving end of a man who has decided to open up to you, then embrace his courage and vulnerability. Thank him for it; praise him for it. Heck, you could even *admire* him for it.

I have learned that the benefits of disclosing my own doubts and vulnerabilities far outweigh those of concealing them. I have also learned that the most strength I can show is the strength and bravery it takes to admit to someone that you are as breakable as they are. Only then can you cast away the shackles of shame that drag you down to the murky depths of your soul and drown you quietly. Only then can you surface again and begin anew.

Finally, I have learned that the greatest sense of security—the greatest protection—a man can provide for his family is love. Remember, love is about giving someone the power to destroy you and trusting they won't use it. It is exactly that vulnerability to potentially being destroyed by someone else that acts as a glue between people who love each other. But you can only truly love others when you learn to love yourself, with all your perfections *and* imperfections.

As for Olivia, I am happy to tell you that today she is a healthy, happy, vibrant young girl. Although she remembers nothing of what happened that day in Italy, she does share a special bond with her Zio Luigi. Every time Luigi sees Olivia—which is usually not more than once or twice a year—his eyes well up with tears. He, more than anyone else, knows just how close a call it was. There is something about seeing such an externally rough, inscrutable, and self-sufficient Mr. Tough Guy melt with emotion like a gelato in the Italian sun. Olivia feels this emotional bond too, even though she doesn't understand why. I guess she will one day, though, when she reads this book.

So, yes, I often wonder what my life would have been like if Luigi hadn't heard those angels whispering in his ear. I also wonder who is the more grateful that he heard those angels whispering—him or me.

I am grateful for all my children, albeit in slightly different ways. I am grateful for Christian, because he was the first and proved to us that "sooner or later, one way or another . . ." I am grateful to Emily, because she defied so many odds, an eight-cell embryonic badass superwoman. And, of course, I am grateful to Olivia, because she proved to me that not only were Trine and I compatible, but I could actually hit a proper duck, rather than just a duck in a petri dish!

What I can say about Olivia, which is a little different from her brother and sister, is that I have never been able to get as angry or irritable with her as I know I have done in the past with her siblings. How could I get as angry, when I know that she is the very manifestation of what my mother used to say to me: 'A vita è bella, pure quanno è brutta.

About the Author

Pellegrino Riccardi was born in the UK into an immigrant family from the south of Italy. A twist of fate while touring in a rock band in Scandinavia in the summer of 1993 introduced him to a young Norwegian who said she was on her way to the UK to study for a master's degree in marketing. They became a couple, decided to move back to Norway together in 1995, and later married. Pellegrino has been living and working from his base in Norway ever since.

Today, Pellegrino is a highly sought-after keynote speaker, conference moderator, and communications trainer. He has three TED Talks to his name, with his talk in Bergen, Norway, on cross-cultural communication reaching more than 1.3 million views.

His unique brand of public speaking has been described as a seamless fusion of masterful storytelling, observational humor, and a potent cocktail of human emotions. These are the very same elements that Pellegrino endeavors to re-create in his writing. Whether you listen to one of his talks or read his books, you will be led on a visceral journey across a wide spectrum of human feelings and emotions.

From a competitive field of more than six hundred of Norway's top speakers, Pellegrino was named Norwegian Speaker of the Year in 2020 by Talerlisten.

Feel free to reach out to Pellegrino on LinkedIn or Instagram by scanning the codes below.

LINKEDIN   INSTAGRAM

Printed in Great Britain
by Amazon

29154656R00164